Write Out Loud

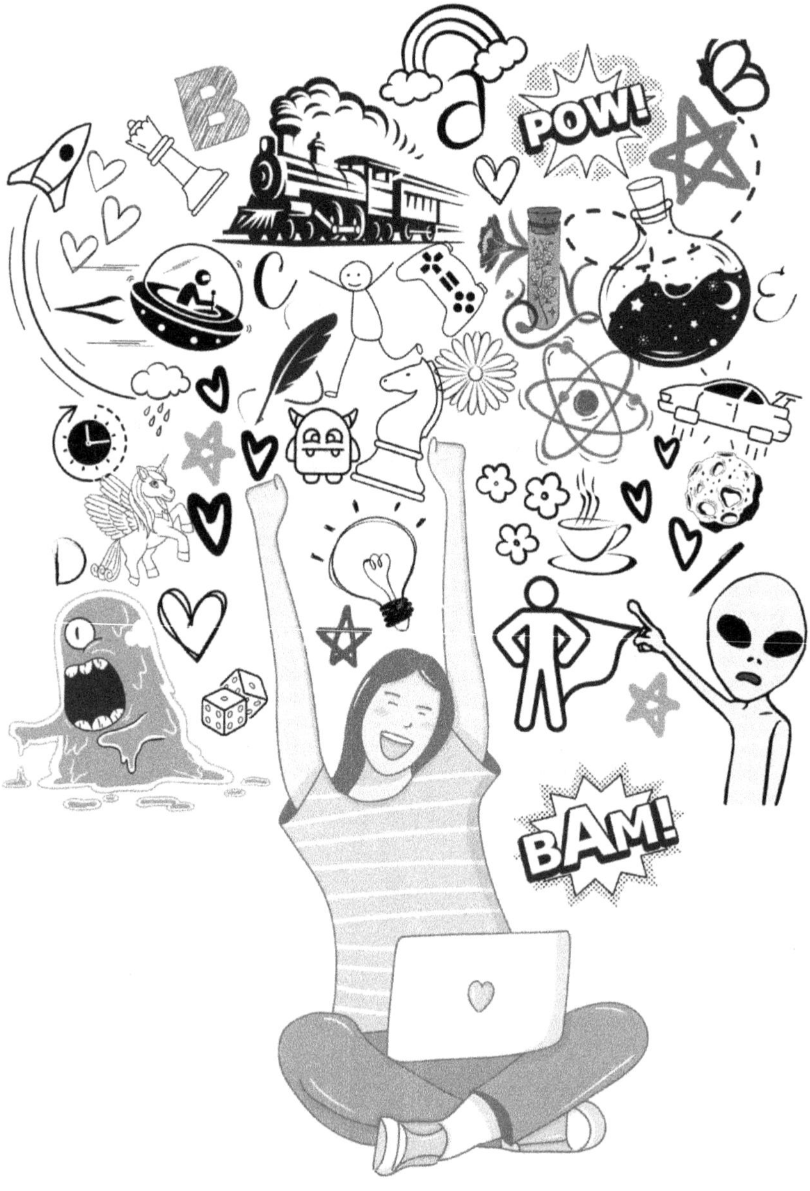
POW!
BAM!

Write Out Loud:

How to Get Over Your Fears and Build the Confidence to Finally Write Your Book

Naomi D. Nakashima

Copyright

Grab Your Write Out Loud Workbook

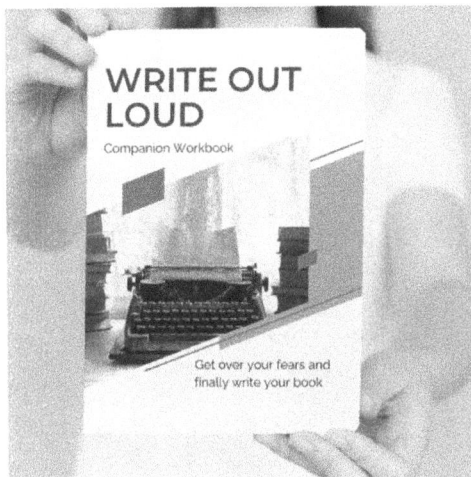

Download this companion workbook to implement everything in this book faster and take the next steps needed to finally get your book published.

Grab your free copy:

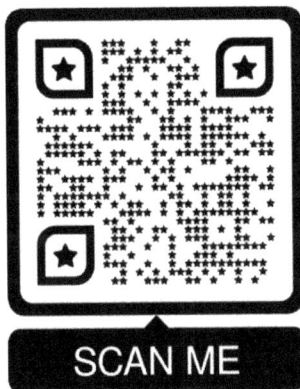

SCAN ME

Dedication

To my two favorite people in all the world—my kids, Piper and Christopher. Never have I met two braver souls who are so ready to take on the world and leave their mark. May you always know and use your voice and never forget that
your story matters.

We are all superheroes in one way or another.

-Jim Kwik, Limitless

About This Book

You'll notice that some of the pages in this book showcase a QR code like this one:

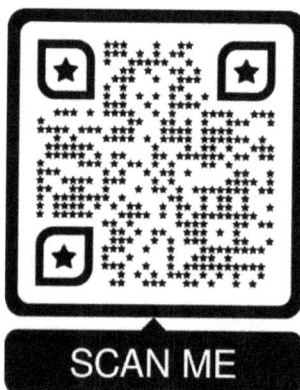

SCAN ME

These codes are here so you can access different worksheets or other tools that I describe in this book and use them to help you write your own book. To scan any of these codes, simply grab your smartphone and open up the Camera App, then focus the camera on the image above the "Scan Me!" caption. Your Camera App will prompt you to go to the page where you can download a copy of that tool.

Please note, the very first QR code I've included is to the Companion Workbook, which includes all the rest of the tools. So, if you download that first one, you don't need to download the rest of these tools. On the other hand, if you don't want the whole workbook and would just like to check out one or two specific tools instead, you can skip that first one and grab the one(s) you want.

Contents

Acknowledgments

I would like to give special thanks to the following people, without whom this book would not exist:

Jim and Laura Rutan, thank you so much for always being in my corner. Even as the rest of the world turned their back, as some of the people I should have been able to trust the most lost that trust, you have always been there with an ear and a shoulder any time I've needed either. Your love and support has meant the world to me over the years and has helped me overcome so much, I don't think I can ever say thank you enough.

Owen and Theresa Hemsath, thank you so much for being two of the most amazing people I know. When my cancer diagnosis came down in 2021, I was buried under thoughts that there was little I could do to set my kids up for their future. All thoughts went to trying to set up the "now" because I didn't believe I had a future. Watching you fight and beat your own cancer diagnosis with such strength and grace inspired me to put in that same fight. I will always treasure our discussions about health, business, and (of course) videos and YouTube.

Akemi Sue Fisher, thank you so much for being such a bright spot in my life. Your passion for business and for helping women find their true voice is apparent in everything you do. Our discussions always made me feel empowered and inspired to get out there and do more, be bigger somehow, find my space, and take it up. I hope you know just how much you inspire me every day.

Molly Mahoney, thank you so much for just being you. You are one of the kindest people I know and somehow always managed to reach out and check on me or even just say hello when I needed it the most. My world is a better place because you're in it and I will always cherish you.

Amanda Elisala, thank you so much for believing in me and for following along my long and winding trail of geekery and shiny objects.

Jessica Cage, thank you so much for coming in and yelling at me every morning. Watching you grow and burst out of your shell over the past two years has been awe-inspiring and you deserve every bit of love, recognition, and adulation that is coming to you right now.

WriterTok, thank you all so much for joining my community and being the bright, positive start to my day every morning. I wish I had the room to name you each individually, as you all deserve so much more than a vague group-paragraph here; but just know that I love you all so much and I believe in you—probably more than you believe in yourself. Keep writing.

Foreword

I met Naomi D Nakashima in the ways of new. That's right. We met on TikTok.

And I quickly became a fan of hers as I watched her present tips to aspiring writers in ways that were encouraging and easily digestible. Don't get me wrong—many people have done this, but Naomi had something special going on. It was the time she took to talk about the side of writing often overlooked; the care a writer must do for themselves as well as their stories.

Soon, I shifted from watching her videos on my FYP to following her, and then to making sure I never missed one of her morning live chats, where I found Naomi had a well of knowledge that she was open to sharing. Not long after that, we were working together on various projects and ideas, and I can truly say I am so grateful that what we all once thought was a silly little dance app came into our lives.

Naomi has built a community around encouragement, support, and openness. Whether on TikTok, Clubhouse, or Discord, the people who follow her get valuable information and they have fun while learning to develop their own talents.

I'm so excited to say that the book Naomi presents brings that same sense of community building and easily digestible content to aspiring writers. All while encouraging them to be bold about their process and let no one tell them that their story isn't worth writing. Write Out Loud focuses not only on writing a book but on the mental care and preparations that writers must take to ready them for the journey ahead. Everyone has a story to tell, and Naomi encourages writers to tell that story unapologetically.

Jessica Cage

Write Out Loud

Introduction

Your Story Matters

Introduction: Your Story Matters

I am never going to get justice for what happened to me. The man who assaulted me is never going to see a day behind bars. Hell, his family never changed the way they look at him.

It's not because I didn't try.

Roughly two weeks went by before I reported, but I did report. Policemen and investigators came to my apartment, cut up my mattress, took photos, grabbed the clothes I wore that day, and brought me down to the station to get my statement on record. They went to friends who were there that night and brought them down to the station to get their statements. And after six months of giving statements and wondering what was ever going to come of anything, the police came back to my apartment and told me that I needed to go back down to the station again.

So, I called into work to tell them I had to go down to the station and I was going to be a little late. Got down the stairs, walked up to the police car, and drove down to the station. They even assured me that once they were done, they would bring me to work so I didn't have to worry about a ride. It was all very casual, which made me feel secure like this was all normal.

At the station, they brought me into a small private room with just a table and a notepad on a clipboard in the middle with two chairs.

A scene right out of a movie.

I don't think my brain has ever been able to fully process what happened next.

After sitting in this room for 20 minutes staring at the table, one of the very same investigators walked in and sat down in front of the notebook and took a deep breath. Then he started telling me a story of a young woman who went on a date. And throughout this date, she had sent a lot of signals to the man that culminated in some, let's just say, spicy material that would have been labeled with three large XX's at Blockbuster. But for some reason, the next day, the young woman regretted her choice of staying with the man. And two weeks later, she found out that the man was married, and she became angry and decided to lie and tell everyone that it wasn't her choice to be with the man at all.

As he told the story, my brain started screaming at me: they don't believe you.

The investigator went on and on for what felt like hours, talking about how many women changed their minds and then seek out to destroy the man's life or get him fired or ruin his career by making up these claims. And he asked me over and over and over again if that is what I did.

And over and over and over again I said no.

He got up and walked out of the room only to come back an hour later eating the remnants of a cheeseburger and sipping on the last bit of soda in his plastic cup then asked me if there was anything else I wanted to tell him. He would ask me if I thought it was fair that so many women were able to get away with lying and get so many innocent men locked up. Did I think it was fair for a man's reputation and career to be ruined simply because a woman regretted her choice?

Of course it's not fair, but that's not what happened.

Eventually, he told me that I had missed my work shift and then he asked me if I wanted to go home.

I took a deep breath, wiped my eyes, and I nodded.

Then he slipped a stack of papers across the table at me and tossed a pen and said all I had to do was sign the papers that would allow them to drop the charges against Tim and I could go home.

So that's what I did.

Because my story didn't matter.

Two weeks later, the same investigator showed up at my apartment again and said he had to bring me down to the station for more paperwork. Just as before, I needed to go to work. And just as before, they said no problem, that once they were done, they would bring me to work.

A voice in the back of my head told me that they had found something, that they had made a mistake, and that they were re-opening the case. And I believed it. I still believed in the system. Besides, what else could it be but that?

So, I followed them to the car. But this time, before I could get in, they took out a pair of handcuffs and let me know that I was under arrest for obstruction of justice and making a false claim of sexual assault. He said he warned me that he was working to stop women from changing their minds and ruining men's careers with the statements just before he pushed me into the car.

At the station, they grabbed my fingerprints, took my mug shots, and they sat me in that same small private room with that same table sitting. And the same investigator came in and threw the same pile of papers on the table in front of me and said, "is this your signature?"

Of course, it was.

He asked me if there was anything I needed to tell him. *Nope.*

Because my story didn't matter.

By now, you've probably been able to guess that the pile of papers the investigator slid over to me and told me that if I signed them, I could go home was actually a statement written up by him claiming that I lied about the whole thing, but it took me longer to work that out. I probably don't need to go into the details about my stay in jail that night, or my arraignment the next morning, or how in my meeting with a public defender he said that only a complete idiot would ever sign a piece of paper without reading it first.

And you probably don't need to know that my public defender fought with me for almost a year in court trying—unsuccessfully—to get the case dismissed because of that signature.

After a year of fighting and continuances, my public defender decided to throw out a Hail Mary and asked me to take a polygraph about the whole experience. Of course! Duh, it seemed so easy, right? The whole case was built on their belief that I was lying, so take a polygraph to prove that I wasn't.

But it still didn't matter.

The judge refused to admit the results of the polygraph. Yet again, my story didn't matter.

After everything, the best my public defender and I were able to do was to settle for a plea bargain that resulted in one year of probation and 500 hours of community service, and in exchange, the records would be sealed so they wouldn't hurt my record as long as I stayed out of the system and didn't get arrested again.

This all happened shortly after my 18th birthday. And I probably don't need to tell you that after this, I didn't exactly trust telling many people things about myself. Even when other women started coming out and making claims against Tim, I didn't step up. I didn't back them up because my story didn't matter.

This is usually about the time when you would learn that I didn't let this stop me, that my story mattered and that I was going to keep fighting until everyone knew it. Unfortunately, it's not that kind of story. I never learned how to look back at this incident and turn it into an empowering branch of my mission.

In fact, I did my best to forget about this story—to push it as far out of my mind as possible.

Now, the truth is, I had no plans on telling the story when I started this book. In fact, this has always been one of those stories that was just gonna come with me to the grave. I didn't see any scenario in which I would ever feel comfortable sharing this story again. It just wasn't a good story: I didn't get justice, Tim was never held accountable, and at the end of the day, I didn't even use my story to help anybody else.

I let my self-pity feed my self-doubt and that stopped me from allowing anyone else to learn from my story. Which, if you have ever worked with me before, you know I wholeheartedly advise against that. Is it any wonder, then, why I've spent so many years trying to help other people tell their stories?

Stories change the world.

And every story has a right to be told.

And the truth is, we all have a story somewhere deep in us that we think doesn't matter. That we think no one else would be interested in, no one else would want to read, no one else would gain any benefit from reading it. But that's a lie.

I don't know how other people can reach my age and say that they don't have any regrets because everything that they have ever done has led them to where they are. Every time I hear someone say that I think to myself about how much I regret signing those papers. I wish I had recognized that my story mattered even then and that I stuck to my guns and refused to sign those papers.

But I didn't—instead, I let them gaslight me into believing that my story didn't matter. And it took me years before I realized that it wasn't true and that my story did matter.

My story wasn't given the chance to change anyone's life. So, the best that I can hope for now is that I can help other authors use their stories to impact someone else's life. And if enough authors get out there and tell their stories, whether they do so as memoirs or through fictionalized retellings, and change the lives of their readers, then we can change the future.

So, no one ever has to feel like their story doesn't matter.

Should you Write a Book?

You probably already know my answer to this question...

Yes! Yes, you should write a book.

Do I need to scream it from the rooftops? Because I will.

Writing a book is huge and scary. And then on top of all that, you never really know until it's done whether or not it's any good or if anyone is even going to like it...so why bother writing a book at all? I can list off half a dozen reasons to write a book without even breaking a sweat, but let's focus on two of the biggest reasons: writing a book is both the most selfish and the most selfless thing you can do with your story.

You see, once you can get over the self-doubt and the stress of writing a book, the writing process itself is tremendously therapeutic. You'll discover more about who you are, and what makes you work, and you'll process some of the many things that have happened to you. You don't even have to be writing about the things that happened to you for writing to help you process them.

Whether you're writing fiction or nonfiction, writing out your story gives you a chance to process your feelings about the world, your perspective on the world, and what you want to share with your audience. Writing allows you to explore your thoughts and feelings about various themes as you shape your story. Even if you don't need the therapeutic effects of writing, just going through this process and exploring your thoughts in this way can help you learn more about yourself you might not otherwise get to discover. And this can lead to a better relationship with yourself and with others.

And, let's face it, writing isn't exactly a team sport. Unless you have small children you're wearing, sitting down to write is something that you're doing on your own for those few minutes. Sure, you can join a group of writers, sign on to co-author a book with someone else, or even schedule working sessions with other writers—but the act of writing itself is a solitary activity, and even if it's just a few minutes at a time, it gives you a break from the conversation with other people for a time. It's time that you can spend on just you: healing, processing, and working through things. Just you and your thoughts.

But you aren't the only one who benefits from getting your story out there. Writing also allows you to share your story with the world. Think of people who would benefit from reading your story:

People who have been where you were but haven't been able to move forward yet due to some unknown issue.

People who have been where you were and have started moving forward but need a little more guidance.

People who haven't been where you were, yet, but might be headed down that path, and could benefit from the warning signs being laid out for them.

People who have been where you were and need to know they aren't alone.

Sharing your story with the world helps ensure that the people who need it the most are able to find and access it at the moment they are looking for it—and what can be more selfless than that? Imagine the impact that your story might have on the next person who is going through, or may go through, the same thing you went through.

Katariina Rosenblatt was a lonely, abused young girl yearning to be loved when she fell into the hands of a confident woman. This woman pretended to forge a much-needed friendship, but in actuality, she was slowly luring her into a child prostitution ring that would keep her trapped for years. Now, Katariina escaped (twice) and went on to heal, she went to school, got a Ph.D., and eventually she wrote her book, *Stolen*.

This book, *Stolen*, does a few things: it tells people how easy it might be for a child trafficker to steal and trap a child in their ring. It gives us a warning about how widespread the issue is and what the real dangers are. But it also provides an avenue of hope for other victims of child trafficking who haven't healed from their torture yet. It shows them that there is hope, that they are not alone, and that there is a light at the end of their tunnel. She serves as a beacon to other victims and to those victims' families that the trauma they've suffered at the hands of the trafficking ring doesn't have to define them for the rest of their lives.

Now think back to something you went through, back at the beginning of that trauma…how easy was it to see that you would come out of it? How much of an impact would it have made in your journey if someone had told you that you weren't alone and that you could follow them out to the other side? Your story, fiction or nonfiction, has the power to give that impact on one of your readers.

Your Book is Your Legacy

When I was a little girl, I had two amazing uncles who had a huge impact on my life. I had my Uncle Jim, who taught me to be fearless and to go out there and live life and not worry about what other people thought. And I had my Uncle Bill, who taught me what it meant to have a voice. Everyone should have an Uncle Jim and an Uncle Bill—those uncles who are way more fun to be around than your parents, they understand you, they believe in you, they tell your overbearing mother to stand down every once in a while, and they teach you things that no one else is teaching you. And I don't mean by standing at a blackboard and teaching you your letters, but teaching you a little bit more about what life is all about. Teaching you the things that are more real than just your letters.

My Uncle Jim lived relatively close by, so we got to see him more often. But my Uncle Bill lived out of state, so every time he came to visit, we made a big deal out of it. The house had to be cleaned and we got new dresses and we got to get our hair done because his visits in and of themselves were sort of a special occasion.

Almost a holiday.

I was almost always one of the first people to wake up in the house. The only person who woke up earlier than I did, usually, was my Uncle Bill. Because of this, I got to spend a little bit more time with him than everyone else. We used to sit at the dining room table and create different things. Sometimes it was puzzles, sometimes it was coloring. Once, he even taught me how to make one of those animated flip books by stapling a bunch of papers together into a book and then drawing on each page the same drawing but just slightly different so that when you flipped through the book it looked like your drawing was dancing.

But there was one morning in particular that has always stood out to me even after all this time. That morning, my Uncle Bill had brought with him these huge pieces of paper—I mean the large paper you can get on a roll there like three-feet-long paper—and this one piece of paper covered the entire table. He pulled out the crayons and we attacked that paper. I had rainbows in one corner, rain clouds in another corner, flying horses, stick people, and just about anything that could cross my imagination found its way onto this paper. When it was all done and there were no more clean spaces on this piece of paper, Uncle Bill looked at me and said, "something's missing."

I studied that paper for what felt like an eternity. I filled in some extra butterflies, some extra birds, and a couple of extra stick people. And he still just looked at this paper and told me, "something's still missing."

So, I went back to it again— this time coloring borders around some of the different drawings so there was no white space left on the paper at all. And then I showed it to him and he smiled, but he still shook his head and he said, "nope. Something is still missing. Do you want me to tell you what it is?"

Of course, I said yes.

He grabbed a black marker and he sat me down at the corner of this huge collage of drawings, and he told me to write my name. That was it, just my name. So, I did. Then he said, "that's what was missing. You didn't leave your mark."

My Uncle Bill was big on making an impact and leaving a mark. He believed nearly any choice you ever made was a part of the mark you were leaving. So much so that he used it as part of his decision-making process: figuring out whether or not that decision was something you wanted in your legacy. Was it something you would want to be known for? Was it something that would make your legacy even better, or would it taint it?

I can still hear his voice, with his smile beaming through from under that cheesy 70s mustache, asking me, *"is this something you would be proud to be known for?"* every time I start to wonder if I'm making the right choice in a matter.

The truth of the matter is you're leaving a mark every time you make a choice. Your book just happens to be a published copy of that mark—your legacy. Every time you make a choice about this book, remember my Uncle Bill and his cheesy 70s mustache, and imagine him asking you, *"is this something you would be proud to be known for?"*

Understanding Your Motivation: What's in it For You?

This thought has been one of the major driving forces behind my entire career, both as an author and as a ghostwriter…*why should I be doing this? What do I get out of writing this book?*

Before you start yelling at me about how selfish that sounds because authors should be in it for the art, I often talk about the *impact* that authors are going to have on their readers. Nonfiction authors, who make up the majority of my clients, tend to already have this impact defined for themselves: they know exactly the type of reaction and impact they're after. They are sharing their expertise, raising awareness of their brand and their solution, and, in some cases, generating leads for their business.

Fiction authors take a little more digging in order to find it, but there's still something in it for them that is more than just "I want to be a famous author." I have fiction-writing clients who are after leading the charge for a more inclusive bestsellers list, others who want to see more and better representation of diverse and differently-abled characters, and others who are reshaping the world into a kinder one through the use of storytelling.

But in both of these cases, the authors are focusing on what's in it *for their readers*. They haven't really started considering what is it in *for themselves*. Are they building a business? Building authority and credibility? Building income? Fame? Clientele? Simply to live in that better, kinder world?

I don't think there is really a bad reason for wanting to write a book, but I do think that it's important to understand what that reason is. First of all, understanding your *why* also makes marketing your book infinitely easier. Your purpose for writing the book becomes the same reason why readers want your book. Secondly, have you ever tried to do something when you didn't really understand why you were trying to do it? If the benefits to you are vague or undefined, then when the difficult times come up, it's a lot easier to quit.

And no one in the history of all the land has ever started writing a book because they wanted to eventually *quit writing the book*, right?

Having a defined goal or purpose, your *why*, gives you a tool for motivation that will help pull you through those times when writing seems too difficult or when you just don't feel like it. And trust me, even if you are excited to write your book now, there will be times when you question this excitement.

Understand What You're Aiming For

What would the world of publishing be without such things as the New York Times Best Sellers list? Or the Wall Street Journal Best Sellers list? Or, really, any best sellers list?

It's hard to imagine because these lists started so long ago, most everyone alive now can't remember a time when there wasn't a best sellers list.

And these lists have helped shape the availability and popularity of books, how we read them, and even when we read them. Even despite the controversy around them, nearly every client I meet with brings up a best sellers list at least once. And nearly every other ghostwriter out there, myself included, and every publisher out there aims to help their clients get onto those best sellers lists—and we use the fact that we have succeeded in attaining a spot on those best sellers lists to sell our services further.

The really sad part about this is that the ability to get onto the best sellers lists has almost nothing to do with the writing at all. Very little to do with the writing and almost everything to do with the *marketing*. And yet every publishing company and ghostwriter out there will use best sellers lists to sell their services to the next author. Every author wishes on a star for that day when they can have a framed copy of their own New York Times Best Sellers list showing their book's title and their name right there in print.

So, believe me when I tell you how hard it is to let go of these best sellers lists. I still use them, I still refer to them, I know how easy it is to buy yourself onto one of these lists and yet I will still tell my clients that it is an absolute possibility. I know that glint in the eye that comes up with the idea of making the best-seller list. But I also want you to believe me when I tell you this: *aiming for a best-seller list is aiming for a fake target.*

I am not sugarcoating when I say it is too easy to buy yourself onto one of those lists. And once you know how those lists really work, once you know just how easy it is to manipulate those lists and once you know what's being done on those lists to help manipulate the public, you can't unsee it. You know that striving for that list is like trying to set an appointment for February 30.

It's a fake target. The day is there, if you showed up at some spot the day after February 29, it will be there. You won't fall off into a void. But it won't be February 30.

So while you are contemplating what's in it for you, why you're writing this book, what you hope to gain from it all, keep this in mind. The best sellers lists are fake, but the impact you have on your life and your readers' lives is *real.*

Identifying and Conquering Your Fears

I'm going to let you in on a little secret: this book is one of the hardest books I've ever had to write. As a ghostwriter over the past twenty years, I have written or helped to write more than twenty-five fiction novels, I have helped to novelize four movies, ghostwritten four memoirs, and ghostwritten nearly forty nonfiction books, workbooks, and guides.

You would think that means I could write this book *on how to write a book* easily. Yet this book is the hardest book for me to write. This book is about finding the courage to tell your story, beating the self-doubt that keeps you from telling your story and being brave enough to finally write your book.

And I am struggling.

So, you might be thinking, *"yeah, Naomi, who the heck are you to tell me to write if you can't even do it?"*

As a person—as a writer and as a freelance writer—I struggle to reconcile with the events of my life and turn them into stories that I can share with other people for entertainment. I have interviewed celebrities, I've survived cancer, survived sexual assault, and I've lived through Operation Desert Storm, Desert Shield, September 11, and the Insurrection on January 6, 2021. I have had two emergency c-sections to deliver two amazing kids into the world after living through an ectopic pregnancy and a miscarriage. I fought my way back out of homelessness twice, I've been at the rock bottom of bankruptcy, and at the height of a six-figure writing career even after being told that I would never make any money writing.

Even after being convinced that my story didn't matter.

My story is definitely not boring. But it doesn't seem to matter how many times someone tells me how exciting my life has been or the amazing things that they think I have done; in my mind I have always battled with putting those things on paper because I couldn't see them as stories.

They were just my life.

Much the same way you are battling with seeing your life as a story now.

The one thing I have always been good at, one of my superpowers, has been helping other people draw their own stories out, overcome self-doubt, and get their books written. How else could I have ghostwritten more than seventy books in my career?

There's a saying that the best doctors often make the worst patients. It's an old proverb centered on the notion that trying to give advice to someone who is a professional in that area is next to impossible. Doctors, with all of their medical training and knowledge, are very difficult to give advice to—they are intimidating because their knowledge is so vast. And quite often, their knowledge is deeper than the person who is trying to give them advice.

Writers work the same way.

Writers have been looking for stories for so long that they can see them anywhere except for the mirror. We can pull the story out of a cardboard box and we will be excited to do it. We are the first to encourage anyone out of self-doubt and struggles—except ourselves.

Go into any writing group on Facebook and you'll see exactly what I'm talking about. Authors—especially new authors—are some of the most supportive people you will ever come across. If you have doubts about your story, they will tell you exactly why your story is amazing and why it needs to come out. If you have struggles writing, they will help you overcome those struggles and give you tips and advice on how to make those struggles seem smaller.

But then, the very next post will be from one of those same advice-givers asking for help because they are struggling with writing, struggling with their story, struggling to see the value in their own story, and fighting self-doubt.

To tell you the truth, it's one of life's hardest ironies.

And one of the worst parts is that the self-doubts—all these fears—don't always go away. Even if you succeed in beating those fears away, even if you get over them long enough to make progress on your book, *the fears come back*. Sometimes stronger than ever, sometimes in a different form, but the fears come back.

So, to answer your question as to *who the heck am I to be writing this book and why should you be listening to me right now*, my name is Naomi D. Nakashima. I have been a ghostwriter for twenty years, and I have been helping CEOs and other authors write and publish their books for all that time. And during that time, I have heard just about every fear about writing books out there. And I have made a career out of helping authors get over their biggest fears and get their books written.

All while having those very same fears myself.

I know the tools that give me reprieve from my fears, I know the tools that have helped my clients, and I know exactly what it takes to draw a story out of someone who is resistant to tell their story because of those fears.

I'm going to use each chapter to dig into a common fear stopping you from writing your book and I'm going to give you the tool you need to work through that fear every time it comes up. Starting with this workbook:

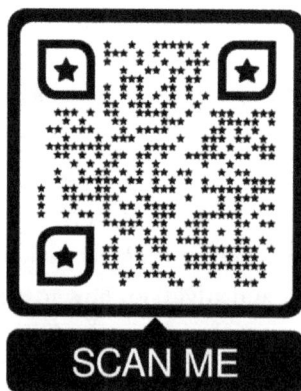

SCAN ME

Your Story Matters

You're just not ready to be called the A-word yet?

Let's just get this out of the way now: the dreaded *A-word*.

Author.

There is a little bit of a debate going on about when a person can start referring to themselves as an author.

On the one hand, there is the belief that authors are published. And for some, not only are authors published, but they are published through the eyes of a gatekeeper (meaning that they went through a traditional publishing process where they found an agent, found a publishing house, and these gatekeepers validated their books and therefore validated their title as an author).

I don't buy it. And neither should you.

I have met some truly astounding authors who have never gone through the traditional publishing process. And I don't mean they tried to go through the traditional publishing process and couldn't find an agent. I don't mean that they took on self-publishing as some kind of a consolation prize. I mean they sat down they looked at the pros and the cons of self-publishing versus traditional publishing and they decided that it was in the best interest of their strategy—the best interest of their *story*—to go ahead and publish it themselves.

No gatekeepers are needed for you to be an author.

Why am I bringing this up this early in the process? Because finding any level of success as a self-published author is a hundred times harder to accomplish if people are not allowed to call themselves an author for cutting out the gatekeeper. It's especially hard to do if you wait until you're already published, traditionally or otherwise, before you start thinking of yourself as an author.

You are an author. Say it out loud.

An author is someone who writes a work *with the intention* of putting that work through a formal publishing process. The key here, really, is your intention. If you waited until after your book was published before you started calling yourself an author, you are going to have a really hard time selling your book to agents and even to readers.

How can you possibly convince anyone that you are an author, much less an author worth reading, if you can't even bring yourself to call yourself *the A-word*?

While I'm ranting about this, there is no need to quantify what level of author you are, either. You are not an *aspiring* author—you made it. You sat down to write a book that you hope to one day see published…your aspirations are over. You made it. You might be stuck, you might be having some doubts, you might be unpublished, but you're doing it. And that's how you become an author, by doing the thing.

And you certainly do not need to quantify this title just to appease some gatekeepers who want to reserve the title for some external validation. Being an author means being your own gatekeeper. You get to decide you are an author, and then you get to do it. You get to decide how you want your career to look, how you want to be published, how you want to spend your time—all of it.

Congratulations, you've been promoted to Author…you're in charge.

You made it.

Building Your Author Persona

One of the first things I start having my clients work on is their *Author Persona*. You know who you are now, as an unpublished author, but who are you as a published author?

Or as a famous author?

People sometimes think that creating an author persona means pulling together a fake personality to act out in public, but the truth is building your author persona is a lot like unlocking a new side of your personality that you might not have been able to reach before. Knowing how you want to portray yourself as a professional author will help you make decisions about what parts of your personal life you should share publicly and which ones should remain private, which part of your journey you want to share, and (most importantly) which part of your persona is the most memorable and relatable for your readers.

Your author persona is closely linked to your author brand, which we will also talk about later. In a nutshell, your author brand sets up reader expectations and how you want to be known, but your author *persona* is who you are online. For example, Stephen King *the brand* brings you into a world gripped by some of humankind's deepest fears and a deep look at how humans react when faced with those fears. But Stephen King *the persona* is a kind, quirky, wise author who wants to see others succeed in a profession he's lived for decades.

By building out your author persona now, you'll find it much easier to recognize yourself as an author...and maybe you'll finally be able to start calling yourself that dreaded *A-word* we talked about.

If you need help planning out your author persona, you can use the Author Persona worksheet I've put together by scanning the QR code below:

SCAN ME

Don't Be Scared by The Success You Find Around You

There are many philosophies when it comes to business and marketing and the mindsets that drive either one. But they all boil down roughly to two primary buckets of thought: scarcity mindset and abundance mindset.

Abundance mindset, sometimes referred to as a growth mindset, is the innate belief that everything happens for a reason and there is plenty to go around. It's the belief that authors are not in competition with each other, but they all have the same goal.

This is the mindset I subscribe to. Books are not in competition with each other; but rather, they are in a relationship with each other. They all sit on the same bookshelf and enhance or in some way better the life of the same reader. When readers head out to a bookstore, the library, or even Amazon, and they start looking up books on a particular subject, they rarely leave with just the one book that won their attention. In fact, I rarely see a reader with just one book on any subject. Most of the time, when they leave that bookstore they leave with an armful of books, sometimes all on the same or related topics and other times on completely varied topics.

Not only that, but they are constantly learning from all the books they're grabbing. They don't read one book and then decide that that's it and that's all they want to know on the subject. They don't read the next book and then decide that it is better than the book they had before and therefore forget everything from the first book. Books don't work like that, and readers don't work like that. When a reader absorbs a book, that story or that information is infused with all the previous stories and information already absorbed. These stories are playing off of each other in the readers' minds, creating cross-references and enhancing the reader's worldview on the subject.

They aren't competing for space inside the reader's mind—they are sharing it.

And once you understand that this is the point of books, it becomes so much easier to see just how your book fits into the bookshelf. It's easier to look at all those other books on the same subject or from the same genre and see where your book fits as well as the type of relationship your book will bring to the bookshelf.

Not only that, but it gets easier to see how other authors succeeding around you could be viewed as proof that it's possible. If there are successful books inside your genre or on your topic. Then that means there is a market demand for the very topic or genre you want to write a book on. How can that be a bad thing?

Sadly, some new authors see how crowded a bookshelf is and they fear it means there is no room on the shelf for their own book. Even the gatekeepers know that there is always room on the bookshelf for another book.

In fact, how many times have you heard other authors talk about being rejected by agent after agent before they finally found one who agreed to represent them? That's not a horror story of mounting rejection: that's proof that it's possible to find representation and get published even after feeling the sting of rejection.

And yet so many authors, especially new authors, don't view these successes as proof of possibility. Instead, they see someone else succeeding and take that as proof of their own failures. They look at another book up on the bookshelf and they see a better writer, a better author, a faster writer, and a better story. They see the acceptance and validation. What they don't see is that this was an author with such perseverance and grit or a team of editors, readers and marketers all working behind them to get that book up on the shelf. What they don't always see is how many times the author was rejected before finally being published.

You

Are A Better Writer
Than You Think
You Are

Who are you, anyway?

When I first started writing, I was under the impression that all that had to happen was I had to think of an idea, and then once I thought of that idea I could sit down and write it. No one warned me that I might ever think I was not good enough for my own ideas.

Yeah, this is exactly what happens to so many authors all the time. Note the sarcastic tone.

If there's one thing I've learned in my twenty years of being a ghostwriter, it's that *you are a better writer than you think you are.*

Ghostwriting, developmental editing, book coaching, and writing coaching all have one important thing in common: *they were all built up as industries because so many authors suffer from imposter syndrome.*

Does this mean that those professions aren't valuable, does this mean that without imposter syndrome we wouldn't need ghostwriters and editors and book coaches? Of course not. We each serve our authors in unique and valuable ways. But our professions would definitely look *very* different if authors didn't have to live with so much anxiety and self-doubt.

Now let me ask you something that I'm sure you've already asked yourself about a million times: other than the fact that it's your story, what gives you the right to tell the story? Who are you?

One of my favorite things about writing and publishing is that anybody can do it. And this is especially true after Amazon 's Kindle Direct Publishing came out and made publishing even more accessible to all of us. However, this also puts us in kind of an awkward spot.

Unlike other forms of skilled labor—such as surgery, doctors, physician assistants, and therapists—there is no formal degree or training required to be an author. To be a university professor, you have to have real-world experience, a master's degree in the area in which you want to teach, and specific training for teaching within the area, but you don't need to have those same qualifications in order to write about that same subject.

So, authors end up in a little bit of a catch-22 scenario. Having a book published is one of the ultimate signs of being an expert. Yet many people do not believe they can write a book until they are already deemed an expert. But there's nobody around to deem them an expert in writing.

Just you.

There's also a bit of guilt that comes with the idea of presuming that your book belongs on the same shelf as the books before it. When I look up at the bookshelf and I see the books that have inspired me over the years—Tony Robbins, Dean Graziosi, Malcolm Gladwell, Neil Gaiman, Jamie Kern Lima, Oprah Winfrey, Jen Sincero, Brené Brown—when I see these books sitting up on the bookshelf and then I think about placing *this* book right up alongside them, there's this feeling of overwhelm and audacity that comes into my head.

Who am I to place my book alongside these great names? *Who am I* to decide that my book is just as helpful or poignant as Shonda Rhimes? Or Stephen King's?

And this is the really funny part about the publishing industry and the book industry in general, is that it's up to me as the author to decide which bookshelf this book is going to belong on. Isn't that crazy? There is nobody else in this world who can decide that my book definitely belongs alongside those other books.

Books have a symbiotic relationship with every other book on the bookshelf. This means, rather than being in competition with each other, they come together to help form influence within a person's mind. Say you read this book and you take the information and you go through the exercises and you start to feel more confident in your book idea, and then you turn around and you read Tony Robbins' book and you gain even more confidence. And then you'll read Jen Sincero's book and gain even more confidence in yourself, in your writing ability, and in your story.

This is the beauty of publishing a book in the world today. I'm not trying to depose anyone; I'm not trying to take over from anyone. I'm not even trying to compete with anyone. What I am trying to do is add to the value they already give you.

But it also feels like anyone in the world could decide that my book does not belong there.

You're not the only one fighting this battle, almost every author I've ever met has come across this very battle: who the heck are they to tell the story?

Even me: earlier I told you the answer to who the heck am I to write this book that you're reading right now. Sure, that was for you and to help introduce you to me and how I can help you and why I am the right person to help you. But it was just as much for me as well because as I picked up this book and started writing, this is the question that was running through my head: *who the heck am I to write this book?*

Now it's your turn.

It's time to figure out who the heck you are to tell your story and why *you're* the right person to tell your story. No one else can ever tell your story the way you can. But if you don't believe me, you can scan the QR code below and fill out the worksheet to find out for yourself.

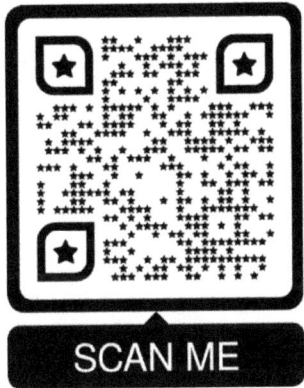

SCAN ME

Developing
Your Book Idea

Developing Your Book Idea

When I was about nine years old, I watched a movie that changed my life: *Romancing the Stone.*

In the opening scene, author Joan Wilder was finishing up her romance novel, tears in her eyes as she banged away on her typewriter to complete her manuscript. She was so proud and blown away by her own novel, she poured herself a glass of white wine and poured some milk into a saucer for her cat to celebrate with her. Both the wine glass and the saucer ended up being tossed into the fireplace as she cheered to her new book.

Then she called her editor at the publishing house and told them of her accomplishment.

But this wasn't the part of the movie that changed my life. This was just the part of the movie that ingrained in me what an author's life must be like (yeah, I know). The part of the movie that changed my life was a little bit later on when author Joan Wilder and handsome, rugged con man Jack Colton were in Columbia trying to rescue her sister.

At one point in the story, Joan and Jack were trying to escape the cartel, which was, of course, hot on their trail. And they were told about a man named Juan who owned a jeep.

So, they traveled to this rather large house to find Juan and his jeep and see about possibly renting the jeep to escape the cartel. As soon as they stepped foot on the property, they were surrounded by people who lived in the area, all of whom were armed and looking dangerous. When they knocked on the door, an unnamed man opened the sliding door and asked what they wanted. Jack responded that they were there looking for a jeep, and the man turned them away.

After being turned away, Jack turned around to face the now dozens of armed men surrounding them and he said, "well Joan Wilder, how are you going to write us out of this one."

At this, the man behind the door re-opened the small peeking door and became very excited.

"Joan Wilder?" he yelled. "*The* Joan Wilder?"

He closed the peeking door and opened the main door with open arms. "I read your books! I read all your books!" He then turned to the rest of the men, "This is Joan Wilder, who writes the books I read to you on Saturdays!"

The men immediately started smiling, nodding, and putting away their weapons as they confessed their admiration in Spanish. Jack and Joan were obviously confused at how her name could have evoked such a reaction.

That was how I learned about the impact that authors had on the world and the moment I knew—I just *knew*—that I wanted to be one. Now all I had to do was figure out what I was going to write a book about!

Unfortunately, it took me years to figure out that next part. Anytime I sat down to write, I was stuck and couldn't think up a good idea. For some of us, that's just what happens: we feel called to write a book before we even have a story to write about.

Fortunately, it's not always as hard as it seems to come up with book ideas.

9 Ways to Come Up with the Perfect Book Idea

Start with the stories you find in art. One piece of advice you will hear me say every time someone tells me that they are blocked or that they are struggling with coming up with an idea is to take some time and *refill their creativity cup*. But you don't have to wait until you've already started writing

Developing Your Story Idea

before you can try this advice out. Sometimes listening to our favorite songs can inspire ideas. I can't even count how many times I have been stuck while writing a client's book. I put on a song, and one line from a lyric can spark an entire story idea. All you need is that thread, then you just start tugging at it.

And there are other pieces of art that you can get ideas from as well. Check out some old photographs and come up with stories behind them. Or some old paintings, you don't even have to go to a museum to see them because you can find a lot of them online. Watch a movie and take one particular scene out of that movie and see if it sparks a new idea for a whole new story. Take the end of an episode from one of your favorite television series and use that as the starting point of a whole new story. Sometimes, I can look up television series online, and check out the episode guide to find the titles of their episodes, and without even watching the show at all, I can find all new ideas just from those episode titles.

Now, I do realize that with these last two ideas, we are getting a little bit closer to fanfiction instead of writing your own book, but fanfiction is not a bad thing. And if that's what it takes to get you started, then go ahead and get started. You'll soon find that your own ideas will start flowing faster than you can possibly record them.

Adapt a story from real life. Fiona Lucas woke up one morning and was scrolling the internet when a new story caught her attention. A man woke up and, after four years of marriage, had no idea who his wife was or why she was in the house with him. That headline ended up being the inspiration behind her book, *Never Forget You.*

We are constantly being bombarded by news and events from our local areas around the globe. Hop online to any news site or social media platform and you will find headlines from the mundane to the bizarre to the completely unbelievable. The stories don't even have to be true for the headlines to spark an idea for a new story. Just start scrolling online and see if one catches your eye.

Adapt the plot of an old legend or fairy tale. I'll be honest, fairytale retellings are some of my *favorite* books to read. Not that there was anything wrong with the originals, although some of them are a bit darker than I think was healthy for me while growing up. I love to see the new perspectives and twists that authors are able to give to these fairytales. For example, Peter Pan, the boy who did not want to grow up—that character became one of my all-time favorites when Robin Williams took to the big screen as a grown-up Peter Pan who could not remember his time in Neverland. What could you do with that? What if Tinker Bell was a queen, what if Hooke was a good guy (or at least not the main antagonist)? What other twists could you add to that story to give it a new life?

Mine your dreams. Not everyone can remember their dreams, but for those people who are lucky or trained enough to be able to remember theirs, sometimes dreams can give you the most wonderfully bizarre sources of inspiration for a new story. If you happen to fall on the unlucky side of that spectrum and can't often remember your dreams, the good news is that there are ways to train yourself to get better at remembering your dreams. It does take a lot of practice, it's not something that you're going to be able to master overnight. But there are plenty of resources available on the internet, and there are therapists and psychologists who specialize in dreams and can also help you.

Brainstorm about the characteristics of a person you know. When Joel and Ethan Coen came up with the big Lebowski, they knew they wanted a detective based on their stoner friend, and that was pretty much all they knew at first.

Sometimes you just need an idea for a great character, and then you can build an entire story around them. So, the next time you're hanging out with some of your friends, take note of some of their personality traits, quirks, catchphrases, or sayings, and start putting together a fictional character based on some of those traits. As you start jotting things down, what ideas start to bounce around, what situation can you see them getting into and how can they get back out of them in an entertaining way?

Write about something that happened in your life. Is there a moment in your life where you can pinpoint a specific impact? Maybe someone said something to you that changed your perspective forever about a particular subject? Or maybe you have a regret that still haunts you to this day. Take a cruise down memory lane and sync back to some of the moments that stick out. They don't necessarily have to be positive or negative memories— once again, we're just looking for a thread to pull at. Did someone say something to you? What did they say and how did it make you feel?

I'm sure you've heard a phrase along the lines of writing the book that you want to read or writing the book that you wish existed when you were younger, and this is one of the perfect ways to get to that idea.

Do some people-watching and discreet eavesdropping. Okay, this one might make you feel a little bit weird, especially if you're like me and you happen to value privacy. But I am not talking about notating every single action that a person takes and writing their life into a book, that would be stalk-y and weird. Have you ever been sitting on a bus or on a bench in a park and just noticing the people around you and making up stories in your mind about what they might be doing, who they might be going to see, where they might be going home from? Just making things up?

Sometimes, this can spark a new idea for a whole new character that develops into an entire plot line for you. And it's the same with conversations. The next time you're sitting in a coffee house, see if you can pick up on any of the dialogue and use that sentence as a starting point for a new scene.

Ask "*what if...?*" There are some people who subscribe to the philosophy that almost every story starts with "*what if...?*" And in a way, I suppose this is true. Even with some of the exercises that I just laid out, a lot of those can start with *what if.*

What if Peter Pan never grew up, what would happen after thirty years of not growing up? What if that valuable lesson you learned when you were 18 didn't happen until you were 27? What if the Titanic did not sink, what kind of effect would that have had on ocean liners and travel? What if humans colonized one of Jupiter's moons? What if Tsar Nicholas II had survived the massacre in the basement? The man who woke up one day with no memory of his wife, what if that had been on purpose because his wife was a spy?

With almost any prompt out there, you can ask the question *what if*, tweak one or two key aspects of that prompt, and come up with an infinite number of other prompts that you can start diving into.

When all else fails, look for writing prompts. There are hundreds, even thousands, of writing prompts available for free on the internet and inside writing groups. There are also dozens of books available on Amazon and other bookstores all designed to help give you that initial spark of an idea. Some of them are just the same *what if* questions that we just covered, some of them go into more detail, and some of them just start with dialogue or a basic premise.

And you may not even end up using them, but sometimes just reading through a series of writing prompts can be enough for you to mash them together into your own prompt or come up with something completely different on your own.

One Rule

Never, Ever Censor
Your Ideas

One Rule for Coming Up with Your Book Ideas

I don't like a lot of rules when it comes to writing books. I find that rules usually just get in the way and block creativity. Most of the rules are best left for editing. That said, there is one major rule you absolutely need to follow when it comes to developing your book idea: *never censor your ideas.*

Don't—*do not*—pre-judge your idea before you've had a chance to flesh it out. I run into so many authors who have a basic idea—a premise or even just a character—and they toss it out before they really know much about it. How? How can you do that? You're already struggling to come up with ideas, and now you want to throw away an idea that might actually work just because you can't see the big picture yet?

There is no way to truly judge whether or not that idea would make a good book if you don't explore it.

1. It doesn't matter if it's a similar concept to a book or movie that's already been done (how many vampire romance novels are out there already? And I literally *always* want more).

2. It doesn't matter if you don't know much about the subject: you can learn as you go. *Experts don't become writers, writers become experts.*

3. It doesn't matter if it seems too "out there" to be any good. If I had been in that pitch meeting when Thunder Levin said "*hey, let's do a movie about a tornado with sharks in it in LA...*" I would have said absolutely not, no way. And I would have robbed a good chunk of the population of their favorite inside joke on the big screen. No matter how bizarre you think your idea is, if you put it together well, you can get a great story out of it and there is always a market for a great story. Or for an inside joke turned into a story, anyway.

4. It doesn't matter if it doesn't make sense right now. Our brains rarely flow from one thought to the next in a usefully coherent pattern. Remember the last time you were hanging out with one (or a few) of your best friends and talking about just whatever random thing came up? How long before one of you stopped and realized you had no idea how you went from talking about all the things

Developing Your Story Idea

wrong with the MCU to talking about the different ways you can get a hot dog in the United States? You may not be able to connect all the dots just yet, but that doesn't mean they won't connect—so don't go throwing any of those pieces out.

As long as you remember this golden rule of ideation, you'll soon find that you actually have plenty of ideas you can write about, you just need to work on a plan to start exploring them so you can narrow them down. And for this, I like to start with a good old-fashioned brain dump.

A brain dump is a really messy name for an amazing organizational tool, only instead of organizing your folders or your notebooks, with a brain dump, you're actually going to be organizing your *thoughts*.

Start with your favorite notebook (or you can grab my brainstorming worksheets by scanning the QR code on this page) and your favorite pen, and grab a timer (yes, your phone can work for this if you are good about ignoring those notifications; but if not, then you can grab any egg timer or kitchen timer) and just start scribbling.

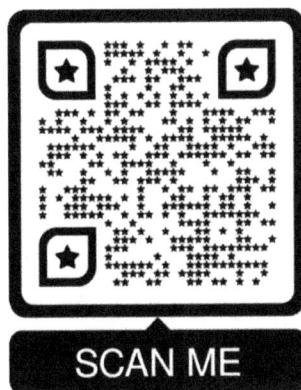

SCAN ME

Every thought that comes into your head, jot it down. Remember what I said: *no censoring*. That means no filtering, no sorting, no judging...just jot them down into that notebook.

What this does is it gives you a physical copy of all the thoughts going on inside your head. Of course, not every thought is going to make it into your book, right? So, the next step is going to be to start sorting these physical copies of your thoughts into two piles:

1. Yes, I want to explore this idea more for this book, or
2. Maybe not, I can't tell if this fits with this idea or might be in a future book

Notice how I still didn't say "no" or use subjective piles like "good ideas" and "bad ideas"? That's because at this stage you still don't really know. An idea that you dismiss this early in the process might just end up being the one you settle on later if given the chance to really explore it.

Once you've got your ideas sorted out a bit, you can start exploring them a little deeper. Take some time to consider each idea carefully, asking yourself questions about each one until you feel you can't go any deeper. Then move on to the next idea and start asking more questions.

Chances are, you won't have to go very far with this before your book idea will jump out at you. And once it does, remember to write down the idea as well as how you got there. I meet authors all the time who will tell me that they wrote down this great idea they had for a book, but then when they went to go start writing it and read their own scribbles, they had no idea why they thought it was such a great idea or what they had planned on doing with it.

If you can, try to download the entire thought process from your brain into a single document on your computer or on your phone. Just open up a document in MS Word or Google Docs—use a notes app if you prefer—and get that premise down in writing. Trust me, you'll be glad to have the whole thought down in one place once it's time to actually start writing.

What if You have too Many Story Ideas?

Picture this for a moment: you get an idea for a book.

It's exciting and you can't wait to get started on it. But then you sit down at your laptop and you struggle a little bit—you can't quite get it to start. Maybe you talk to a few people, maybe do some research or you hit up

Pinterest for a writing prompt or something to help you get over that first little slump. And eventually, you're able to start putting everything together and *finally* get working on your book.

And then it happens... *Another book idea strikes you.*

And then another one.

And then *another* one.

And before you know it, you've got 10 book ideas all floating around and getting tangled up in your thoughts and keeping you from being able to focus and write on just the first one you started. They might even be making your first book idea seem a little vague or amateurish or downright bad. Maybe your first book idea is now looking a bit boring.

Of course, it's not boring. It's the same exciting book idea it was when you first started writing it. It's the same book idea you fought so hard to get started on. So how can it be boring? Why do these new ideas all seem more exciting?

Creativity is an amazing tool. Once you start using it, you can't run out of it. In fact, the more you use it, the *more* you will gain. So it makes sense that as you finally start working on that first book idea, all these other ideas would start flowing into your mind. Once you have unleashed that creativity, it's going to *over*flow through you.

The good news is that you don't have to choose one story over another. That initial hit of inspiration is exciting, but it doesn't mean that the original story idea is *less* exciting or is suddenly bad or boring. What it does mean is that this new idea has just given your brain a huge boost of dopamine and you want more.

But my rule still stands: *never censor your ideas*. When these new ideas start flooding into your head, rather than trying to block them out just so you can focus on your first idea (or worse, abandoning your first idea in favor of one of these new ideas), open up a new document and jot down the premise of this new idea along with any notes you might need to remind yourself of your exact inspiration.

Don't get sucked down the rabbit hole of researching and outlining this new book idea just yet. Downloading these ideas from your brain into a document can usually get them out of your way so you can get back to working on your primary story within a day or two.

Self-Publishing, Traditional Publishing, or Somewhere in Between: Marking Your Path

It's a question that comes up in nearly every writing group around the internet, during nearly every client call I have ever had, and during every group event I've ever attended: *which is better, self-publishing, or traditional publishing?* It's a question that every new author wants to know the answer to.

But it's not an easy question to answer. This is such a loaded question because the truth is that neither one is better than the other. Traditional publishing has been around longer and has had more time to develop a positive reputation, while self-publishing was once relegated to rich people who didn't want to navigate the gatekeepers and could afford to go around them and put a book out. Then, once Amazon's Kindle Direct Publishing came onto the scene, the Amazon bookstore was flooded with mediocre, and sometimes downright bad, self-published books that were very low quality and easy to spot on the website.

And many of those books were only published through KDP because those authors were *not* successful in finding an agent willing to publish the book through traditional means. In fact, of KDP's 15-year history, the first 5 years of was flooded with these bad books, meaning that self-publishing has *only had about a 10-year history as a solid alternative to traditional publishing.* But what a decade it has been!

Now, the choice between self-publishing and traditional publishing has nothing to do with gatekeepers or whether or not you *could* get published traditionally. (This is actually one of my pet peeves, whenever I hear someone say *don't worry, if you can't find an agent, you can always turn around and self-publish later.* Self-publishing has grown beyond being a consolation prize for writing your book). Today, the choice between self-publishing and traditional publishing comes down to strategy, timing, and the type of experience you want as an author.

Traditional publishing allows you as the author to focus on writing and marketing your books *and that's it*. You write the book; you send it off to a publisher who gets the book edited and formatted while you go online and tell your readers about the book. You never really have to worry about hiring an editor, finding a formatter, or interviewing a book cover designer, the professionals at the publishing house have got you covered there. So, your career as an author allows you to focus on just being the author.

You may have guessed, but self-publishing is the opposite of this. With self-publishing, you become the *publishing company*. So, not only are you writing the book, but you are also handling the editing, the formatting, the cover design, and any illustrations that come with it, as well as marketing the book and getting it in front of your readers. How you choose to do this is up to you, whether you hire an editor, or edit the book yourself, whether you hire an illustrator with publishing experience, or hire your brother. All of those choices come down to your vision for the book, your budget, your timeline, and your skill set. In this way, self-publishing is a much more entrepreneurial experience than traditional publishing: you are literally launching a business as a publishing house with yourself as your first and only client.

Of course, this isn't the only difference. Timing also plays a big part in which path is the better path for your book. For example, self-publishing is a faster road to publication. With traditional publishing, not only are you taking the time to query agents but even once you find an agent willing to represent you, there is the time it takes to sell your manuscript to a publisher. And once that manuscript has been accepted, the publishing process itself can still take anywhere from one to two years before you see that book on shelves. With self-publishing, you can set the timeline and get that book up in just a few days (although to be clear, *I don't recommend ever throwing a book up in just a few days*).

Because of this glaring difference, if your book is time sensitive, or if you are trying to be the first onto the scene with a particular project, self-publishing will give you a clear advantage over traditional publishing.

And not only is the publishing process faster with self-publishing but payment and marketing are also typically faster as well. With traditional publishing, you usually get paid about twelve to eighteen months after a sale. This means, if you tried a new marketing strategy in January, you wouldn't have access to the sales analytics to let you know whether or not it worked, and you would only be able to measure the success of that marketing strategy when you got your royalty payment, which would be in January of the next year or possibly as late as June of the next year. And that's if you aren't paying back an advance and are actually being paid your royalties.

With self-publishing, you typically get paid your royalties within thirty days, and the analytics and results of your marketing strategy are available to you almost immediately if you have your platform set up correctly.

So, speed and timing definitely play a huge part in choosing a publishing path. The bad news is that this choice can sometimes feel overwhelming because there are so many considerations to be made. The good news is you don't have to make this choice right now. And, in fact, even if you did make this choice right now, you can still change your mind back and forth as many times as you like right up until the moment you either hit publish on a self-publishing platform or sign a contract with a publishing house.

And even then, with some luck and a really good reason, you might still be able to change your mind even after signing.

You're probably wondering why I'm telling you all this and spending all this time discussing the differences between self-publishing and traditional publishing this early in the book if you don't even have to make this decision yet? I'm telling you all this because it's usually one of the first questions someone asks me, right behind how to come up with a book idea and how much money they can make as an author. So I want to put your mind at ease. You don't have to know all this now.

But if you already have your mind made up or if you're leaning in one particular direction over another, then what you do right now can set you up to make things easier down the road.

For example, a major piece of your query letter when you're trying to get traditionally published is going to be your author platform: how big your reach is across social media and other channels. The size and activity of your author platform help agents and publishers determine just how much help you'll be able to give when it comes time to market and sell your book. This means you'll want to start building this author platform sooner rather than later as you'll need to have it built up before you can start querying.

On the other hand, if you're planning on self-publishing, you don't need to start building your author platform while you're still writing. You'll still want to start building your author platform before you sell your book, but you can wait until it's written if it's not something you're comfortable doing now.

Your publishing path can also make a difference in how you write your book and what you decide to include in your book. When you are traditionally published, that publisher owns the pages of that book. Sure, the intellectual property and all the ideas are yours, but the real estate—the space on the pages itself—belongs to them. And they are in charge of how that space is used and presented. Most people take that to mean the overall formatting; and that is part of it, but it also includes things like links or QR codes to other content.

For example, throughout this book, I've included several links to other resources you can check out or sign up for—this allows me to write the book and suggest resources without having to take up time and space explaining how to use those resources here. This isn't something that most traditionally published authors are able to do, so they need to write their book as a singular, stand-alone resource. Therefore, if you are planning on traditionally publishing, you'll need to find a way to write a lot of those ancillary resources into your book.

Now, here's the big thing that I want you to remember from all this, and this is one of the most important things for you to remember so I am going to say it again here: *you don't have to make this choice now.*

You'll have plenty of time to make this choice further down the road, so if you're not sure which path you want to take, then congratulations: you're right where you should be.

Settling on a Genre

A lot of authors hate the idea of having to choose a genre. To many of them, the idea of a genre is restrictive and just forces their book idea into a box with a label on it that they may or may not want to venture out of. But genres are not meant to be restrictive, nor are they meant to saddle your book with a label.

A genre is a way of classifying the type of book you're writing, and it's useful throughout the entire industry. Agents use your genre to help sell your manuscript to the right publisher, bookstores use your genre to understand which shelf your book belongs on, and readers rely on their favorite genres to help them choose the book they want to read. Every step of the way, from publishing to reading, relies on understanding how to classify your book in order to know what to do with it.

So, you can see why it's pretty important for you to understand where your book falls into the spectrum, right?

It all comes down to the reader: your reader wants to know what they're getting into when they pick up that book and start reading it. And you can't always know what assumptions they're going to make, either. I was hosting an audio chat room on a social media app called Clubhouse back in 2020 when an author made a comment that their reader should have expected the book in question to be high fantasy because it had dragons in it...

But who's to say that it couldn't have been a horror book with dragons in it? How different do your expectations become when you think about a horror novel with dragons versus a high fantasy novel with dragons? What about a dark fantasy? Fantasy romance?

Not only do genres help set up the expectations for your readers, but they set your book up for success. How many times have you been browsing an online bookstore only to see a review that reads something like "not really my thing" or "I'm not really into this genre…" Sometimes that happens because the reader is trying to branch out into another genre, sometimes that happens because a friend or family member sends them a copy of a new book and they decide to read it out of obligation, and sometimes that happens because reading the book has been assigned as a requirement for a class or a book club or some other obligation. But other times, more than all those other reasons combined, it happens because the expectations weren't set up properly and the book didn't follow the rules of its intended genre.

But Naomi, you said you didn't like rules when it came to writing. There my words go again, biting me in the tail.

I don't like a lot of rules when it comes to writing, but one set of rules I do follow is understanding the genre I am trying to write in so I can manage those expectations, set up a marketing campaign that targets the right readers, and help my clients and their agents approach the best publishing houses for their books. I like to choose my genre first and then write the book that falls in line with that genre, but you can absolutely just write the story in your head first, then try to figure out which genre it fits into and make any adjustments to help ensure that it belongs.

What goes into a genre? What makes a fantasy book a fantasy book instead of a historical fiction book? Turns out, there are a few things to consider when it comes to choosing a genre:

The emotional experience you aim to give the reader. This is one of the most critical pieces to consider when choosing a genre. Even books with similar elements can give readers very different emotional experiences. Remember how I said I love a good fairytale retelling? How different would a horror book with Little Red Riding Hood be than a fantasy romance book with Little Red Riding Hood? Even a dark fantasy book with Little Red Riding Hood wouldn't give the same emotional ride that a horror book would give. And all of these would give a very different emotional experience than a romance novel would give, even if they had romantic elements within them.

The medium, length, or format of the story. I probably don't need to tell you that long stories read very differently than shorter stories, which also read very differently from illustrated stories. Take a minute to think about your favorite book, then imagine how it might read if you were to cut that book in half. How much more focus would be on the action rather than on the character development, the inner struggles, or the overall emotional state of the characters? Quite a few fantasy novels would end up reading more like adventure books if you had to cut out a lot of the history, lore, and descriptions that go into building a fantasy world and chose to focus solely on the elves and the battles.

Speaking of world-building, where the book takes place. Setting alone is never enough to fully determine a book's genre, but it is a good starting point. Does your book take place in the American Old West? Does it take place sometime in the future? On a spaceship? Under the ocean?

There are dozens of genres, and when you add in overlapping elements and subgenres, the list gets even longer and more complicated. So, it's no wonder genre feels so unimportant when all you want to do is sit down and write your story. But I encourage you to at least give some thought to the type of genre you're aiming for, if for no other reason than to give you something to tell your prospective agent when you're trying to query for publishing later. If you're not sure what your genre is, you can scan this QR code to grab a worksheet to help you narrow it down a bit.

SCAN ME

12 Genres and Their Rule of Thumb

Now, I don't want you to start getting obsessed with the idea that you have to know every single genre inside and out before you can start writing your book. There is plenty of wiggle room and you can always, *always* fix anything that goes too far outside of your genre during editing. But if you know some of the basics of the genre while you're writing, it's a little easier to stay close to that framework.

So, just what are the expectations set forth by each genre? Here is a brief summary of each of the most popular genres.

Genres in Fiction

Adventure: an adventure novel focuses on just that, the adventure. This is a quest or journey as the central focus of the plot. And the journey itself is fast-paced and action-packed. In an adventure novel, the characters' physical journey, how they change through the adventure, is as big a focus as the journey itself.

Contemporary: A contemporary novel is just as the name describes: a story that takes place at the same time the reader is living in with the conflicts and issues taking place within the character's life.

Dystopian: A dystopian novel is one in which the government has, through either deliberate action or inaction, brought about the fall of civilized society, leading to widespread misery, oppression, environmental destruction, or constant war. In a dystopian novel, the protagonist is usually one person, or a small group of people, who go against the human psyche of the time. They aren't exactly leading a revolution, but they are lighting the spark.

Fantasy: The term fantasy is so broad that it actually encompasses several genres, so it's no wonder it's one of the most popular book genres available. At its core, a fantasy novel contains magic. The magic can be a person using magic, such as a wizard or a warlock, to enact change around them, or it can be the existence of magical creatures such as dragons and elves (or both).

Historical Fiction: A historical fiction novel is any novel set at least fifty years in the past with a plot that intertwines with historical events. One of the most common questions I get about writing a historical novel is on historical accuracy; let me put this mess to rest. Your historical fiction novel is a construct, just like any history book. It is written with your perspective and bias in mind. This means you can leave doubt as to what "really" happened. However, you can't invent a new history. In other words, you can add events, people, and conversations around a known event, but you can't alter the event itself and still have it considered historical fiction.

Horror: A horror novel centers on something terrifying. This genre is often coupled with a thriller, which focuses heavily on the suspense aspect of a novel. The primary difference between the two is that the goal of a horror novel is to horrify or scare the reader, while the goal of a thriller is to thrill the reader. Another distinguishing factor between the two is the catalyst. Because a horror novel is working to horrify the reader, the catalyst that sets events in motion is typically outside of the protagonist's control, they happen to be at the wrong place at the wrong time, and as a result, they become a victim of happenstance.

Mystery: A mystery novel is, as the name suggests, a novel whose plot focuses almost entirely on a mystery that needs to be solved and the protagonist who is involved in solving it.

Paranormal: A paranormal novel is set within a realistic world and includes events and beings that are beyond the typical scope of scientific understanding, such as ghosts, poltergeists, or vampires.

Romance: The romance genre is both its own, stand-alone genre with its own rules and a subgenre that can be included as an element in nearly any other genre. In its own genre, a romance novel is defined by the focus on the romantic relationship in addition to the characters and plot. The goal of a romance novel is to help the reader fall in love with the characters as much as they fall in love with each other. And a romance novel always has a happy, optimistic ending. When used as a subgenre within another novel, the relationship becomes a device to introduce intrigue or conflict into the plot rather than a driving factor of the plot itself.

Science Fiction: A science fiction novel includes a futuristic setting and society that have developed and use advanced technology to our own. Like romance elements, science fiction elements can be added to other genres, such as the use of time travel to get into a historical fiction novel, using the fall of society as either the result of advanced technology or as a catalyst to build advanced technology in a sci-fi, dystopian novel, or using a scientific source of magic in a sci-fi, fantasy novel.

Teen Fiction / Young Adult: Young adult novels are characterized by the age of their primary protagonist, which is typically between 13 and 17 years old. These novels focus more on the emotional development and inner struggles of the protagonist, creating a character-driven story rather than a plot-driven story.

Contrary to popular opinion, young adult novels are not necessarily exclusive to teen readers. In fact, a lot of adult readers enjoy reading young adult novels. However, considering the age of the protagonist and the focus on emotional development and struggles, many of the issues within these novels tend to stick to issues suitable for teenagers.

Thriller: Thriller novels are often lumped together with horror because the aspect of scaring the reader is often thrilling, but thriller novels tend to focus more on the suspense that leads up to the scream than on the scream itself. In thriller, the authors focus on anticipation. The catalyst, the spark that sets events in motion, also plays an important part in distinguishing the thriller novel from the horror novel. I mentioned earlier that in a horror novel that catalyst is usually outside of the protagonist's control, but this isn't usually the case in a thriller novel. Most of the set up within a thriller novel starts with the protagonist learning about something terrifying, usually a warning of some kind, who then proceeds further and kicks off the events without paying heed.

Genres in Nonfiction

Cookbook: The cookbook is a fairly self-explanatory genre; a book whose primary focus is to share a collection of recipes. While many cookbooks differentiate themselves within the genre by including histories and personal stories, the focus of the book, the primary goal, is to share the recipes with the reader.

Development: A book on personal development focuses on helping the reader generate and nurture a change in their character or mindset. Because development books are often released with the promise of helping readers improve their lives. In some ways, these books get lumped in with the more general self-help books, but the focus on improving the self in order to improve your life is the main focus and differentiator for the development book.

Families and Relationships: The focus of a family relationship is just that: families and relationships. This may include dating books, marriage advice, or parenting advice. These books are often written by people holding education around such relationships, such as therapists and psychologists, but there are also a number of books available written by people drawing experience from their families and personal journeys rather than formal education.

Health: A health book is as the name suggests: a book on health and overall wellness. This can mean physical health as well as mental health, nutrition, and fitness; and while having a formal education in any of these areas can help build credibility behind your book, it's not a requirement in order to write a book about any of these topics. For example, a nutritionist can write an amazing book on nutrition and dietary lifestyle that helps thousands of people who are struggling with health problems related to their nutrition. Someone who has changed their dietary lifestyle and lost a significant amount of weight and has been able to keep it off, with or without the help of a nutritionist, could also write and publish a book chronicling their weight-loss journey, and what worked for them. Either way, the author should take care to remember that not every bit of medical advice will pertain to every case and, of course, readers should be encouraged to seek medical attention when they need it, rather than taking the advice out from a book as medical advice.

History: A history book chronicles events that took place in the past and sometimes analyzes the impact of those events on the present. In some cases, the actual chronology of an event might be lost or misunderstood, and so sometimes the accuracy of these events may be off or left unknown. But the goal of the history book is to help the reader build a new understanding of the event in question and, if possible, increase their understanding of how that event has helped shape an aspect of their life.

How-To / Step-by-Step Guide: The how-to book or guide is pretty self-explanatory. This is a book that walks a reader through a process to complete a goal or task.

Memoir: A memoir is a book in which the author chronicles certain parts of their life in order to help the reader extract significant lessons that they can apply to their own life to find a solution or overcome obstacles.

Motivational: A motivational book is a book that has been written with the sole purpose of uplifting the reader and compelling them to take action in some aspects of their life or business.

Self-Help: Similar to a book on development, the self-help book aims to help people improve their lives, in whole or in part, while also empowering them toward a positive change. The primary aspect that sets a self-help book apart from a development book is the catalyst leading to these improvements within the reader's life. In a development book, the focus is on the reader improving some aspect of their mindset or character in order to enact a change that will benefit their life. In a self-help book, the focus is on helping a reader help themselves by learning skills or gaining a new understanding of a complex topic. For example, a self-help book on decluttering and organization might help the reader by teaching them quick tips and hacks they can use to declutter their house within a few minutes, but the development book will help them solve the issue around cluttering by helping them to understand why they allow clutter to build up in the first place and how their relationship with the objects cluttering their home is keeping them from being able to let them go.

Travel: Books on travel typically help readers understand various regions around the world, tourist attractions, or experiences they might expect when planning a trip themselves.

Teen Nonfiction: Most nonfiction books can be read by teens without really causing too many issues. However, teen nonfiction books tend to perform better when you focus your attention more on the emotional struggles rather than the outward advice. When young adults believe that you can understand how they are feeling, they are more likely to follow the advice given to them, but if you just start throwing advice at them without establishing that emotional connection, they have a tendency to tune you out more often, even if the advice that you are given is proven and would normally be something they would be open to trying.

Establishing Your Premise

There are dozens of plotting formulas and structures available for you to choose from, and to be honest, I don't think one is better than the other. Like most anything else right now, your writing journey is going to be a very personal experience—built by you using tools and strategies that work for you. And chances are, some of those formulas won't feel right to you; they won't feel like they are doing justice to your story, you won't feel a connection to them, or you'll find yourself trying to tell your story in a different way that just doesn't align within your chosen formula.

And that's fine.

One thing you do want to map out before you start looking at these plot formulas is your premise. Your book's premise is a short, usually just one to two sentences, explanation of your story that sets up the reader's expectations and helps you stay on target. In other words, it's a quick and dirty summary of the book you're trying to write. And no matter what genre book you are writing, no matter which path of publishing you plan on taking, and no matter what plotting structure you are choosing, you absolutely should write your premise first.

A lot of people think of the premise as a sales pitch. And it can be used to pitch your book idea to agents or readers, but it also does so much more than that:

Your premise will help simplify your book idea

If you have spent any time online in the past three to four years, then I know you're going to recognize how powerful *simple* can be. How many times while you were creating a video for TikTok or snapping a photo for Instagram did you put so much energy into that content only to be met with very few views? And then, you're scrolling through your favorite social platform, and you see content that looks like it had been just thrown together with nary a thought or plan, practically on a whim, and that content is getting hundreds of thousands or even millions of views. It's not because the algorithm doesn't like you, it's not because your lighting isn't perfect or your sound quality is bad—it's because at the core of everything we do online, *we do it to be entertained.* And if at all possible, we want to be entertained without having to think about what we just watched. We want to learn new skills and build a new mindset in an entertaining way that keeps us engaged and doesn't *feel* like we're "*learning.*"

I come across new authors all the time who want to add surprises, plots, twists, and basically the kitchen sink into their books. And there's nothing inherently wrong with wanting to throw the kitchen sink into your book, provided that we are still talking about a proverbial kitchen sink and you aren't actually about ready to toss a stainless-steel sink at your computer, but how do you know when enough is enough? How do you know where to draw the line about which plot twist and which surprise is adding to the entertainment value of your story and which plot twist will make the reader's eyes roll?

This is where having the premise broken down can be so valuable for you. If you can break your book down into a single promise, then whenever you are wondering whether or not to add in that next twist, you can look back at your premise to help guide you in that decision.

Your premise will help you validate your book idea

Have you been wondering whether or not your book idea is even a good one? Are you trying to decide how much of a market there is for your book before spending weeks or even months trying to write the book?

Your premise will act as a tool for validating your idea before you even start writing the book. You can get plenty of feedback from your community, from your followers, and from other writers by sharing a premise the same way that we would share an elevator pitch.

Most of the new authors I've met over the years have a hard time breaking down their book idea into one or two sentences. When we hop on a call to go over their needs, as soon as I ask them about their book idea, they drone on for five to ten minutes before I even understand what it is they're writing about. And, again, there's nothing wrong with geeking out about your book idea. You should be geeking out about your book idea because it's amazing and inspiring. But if you are looking for feedback on that idea, then you need to be able to boil it down as succinctly as possible.

Your premise will help get you published

If you are looking to be traditionally published, or even if you haven't made that choice yet but you are leaning that way, then your premise will be one of the most important pieces to include in your query letter or book proposal. Just as I said about using your premise to get your idea validated, your premise becomes the foundation of your pitch, so it's helpful if you are able to practice that pitch sooner rather than coming up with it later. The last thing you want to be doing is trying to figure out how to try to boil down your entire book into one simple premise on the fly while you're trying to write your query letter.

Your premise will help you keep your promise

It can be really easy to skip from one thought to the next. In fact, it's easier than you probably think to leave ideas completely out of your book by accident altogether.

I had a client reach out to me about a book they had already published about Twitter marketing for businesses and they wanted to see what they can do to help boost their book sales. So, I did what any other book coach would do: I went and checked out the book. I checked out their marketing content, their blurbs, the Amazon sales page, and every mention of the book that I could find online to help me get a better understanding of the success they thought they should be receiving with this book. And what I found was that the blurbs—the promises that she made for the book—were not actually *in* the book at all.

And this isn't the first time this has happened; it's probably not going to be the last time. It's really easy to sit down and think to yourself "I'm going to write a book that teaches people about budgeting and finance" and then sit down and start writing about your experience and all of your stories, around budgeting and finance, and forget to actually *put in the exercises and the explanations* that would help people learn to budget, and finance.

That's exactly what happened here; she had packed that book with some amazing stories about people she met, networking events she had been to that were facilitated by her presence on Twitter, and the type of growth her business experienced on Twitter. But she forgot to put in the actual steps that new business owners would need to follow in order to follow her road to success. There were no exercises in there, there was no explanation of how these events helped her or how she reached out to some of these other business owners. She didn't even mention the avenues she took when reaching out to other business owners, whether or not she had looked up their email addresses and emailed them or used Twitter's direct messaging service. Only that she found clients on Twitter.

Putting together a premise helps you avoid these types of complications when you're writing your book. It serves as a North Star— you can always go back and refer to it to make sure you are on track and fulfilling your promise. And, of course, it also allows you to change the track, change your promise, should you need to if you choose to leave something out.

The 5 Elements of Your Premise

In fiction, your premise can be broken down into 5 major elements: the main character, the situation they are in, their personal objective, their primary opponent, and the disaster their opponent created in order to stop the main character. Broken down into a formula, the premise will look something like this:

[Main Character Name and Descriptor], sign up to [situation]. [Pronoun] just wants [personal objective], but [opponent name and descriptor] is forcing [disaster].

A premise works much the same way in most nonfiction books. The primary difference between writing a premise for a fiction book versus writing a premise for your nonfiction memoir or guide is that instead of the main character, you and your reader share the role of the main character. Besides that, the rest of the elements still apply: the main character (you and your reader), the situation you were in before you found the solution to your problem (that your book is going to help your reader learn), your personal objective [and why it was so important for you to implement this solution], their opponent or obstacle to implementing that solution, and the disaster or the cost of what it might mean to your reader if they don't overcome this obstacle.

You can then add another sentence highlighting the solution. Broken down into a similar formula as before, the premise for a lot of nonfiction books will look something like this:

[I was or You are and descriptor] struggled with [situation]. I was tired of [personal objective], but [opponent] and [disaster]. Learn [solution] without [struggle].

And before you throw this book across the room and start yelling at me about how hard it is to boil down your entire book idea into just a couple of sentences, trust me I *know*. I absolutely know. It's like trying to pack an entire summary of the complete Star Wars saga or the entire Lord of the Rings trilogy into a single paragraph.

It's *hard*.

This is all the more reason to try to write it now, or at least start thinking on it a bit, before you pack your brain with all the things you're about to write about.

The Premise is an important part of what I call your book's North Star; and if you'd like some extra help with writing your premise (and the other points of your North Star), you can scan the QR code on this page to grab a handy worksheet I've put together for you.

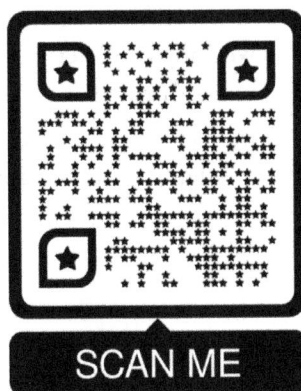

SCAN ME

Examples of a Premise in Fiction

When Katniss Everdeen, a survivalist by necessity, volunteers to take part in a televised fight to the death, she just wants to survive and return home to her family. But the game makers change the rules at the last moment, forcing her to choose between killing her best friend or letting her best friend kill her.

When the angel Aziraphale and the demon Crowley develop an unexpected friendship and grow comfortable with their lives on earth, they decide to interfere with the Antichrist's upbringing and avoid Armageddon from ever happening. But when a series of misunderstandings result in the wrong child being monitored and the real Antichrist growing up unwatched, the Four Horsemen of the Apocalypse set to work bringing about the end of the world and recalling the two back to their respective homes in Heaven and Hell.

Examples of a Premise in Nonfiction

New authors looking to make a full-time income with their storytelling need to learn business strategies, but those resources are generally hard to find and take a lot of time. Learn the skills and strategies here without pulling out your hair.

As a new mom, I struggled with trying to fit all my responsibilities into my day. I was tired of missing important deadlines and feeling guilty about not spending as much time with my daughter as I wanted, but every time management system I tried seemed to fall short and increase my anxiety rather than actually help me get a handle on my schedule. Learn how to put together a time management system that works for the way your brain is wired and stop feeling guilty when someone else's system doesn't work for you.

Validating Your Book Idea

No one likes the idea of working hundreds (or thousands) of hours developing a new product only to watch that product sit on store shelves collecting dust ignored by the world at large because no one else wants or needs it. Nobody has time for that! So, validating that book idea and ensuring you know the market of people who are most likely to need and buy it before you start writing just makes sense.

There are three key elements to consider when validating your book idea:

1. Does it have an existing audience or market demand? Is there a market for the type of book you're selling? If there are books already out in your niche or genre that are selling, that's a pretty good indication of current demand. There are plenty of tools available to help you see just how many people are searching for certain types of books, but you can also use Amazon, a powerful search engine in its own right, to find out how books are doing without paying for any of those tools. While Amazon won't tell you exactly how many copies of a book they've sold, you can start to get a pretty clear picture as you check the sales ranks from several books in that genre.

If you can't find anything similar to your book at all, take a moment to reflect on why that is—is it because you are a pioneer blazing a trail into the undiscovered territory? Or is it because you are looking at the wrong genre or that you have hopped onto an idea others ignored for a reason? Most of the time, when an author tells me that there is *nothing* like their book at all out on the market, we can usually find something pretty close just by adjusting our search terms.

2. Is that audience willing to pay? This applies more to nonfiction books than it does to fiction books, but if there is a market out there that needs your solution or training, are they willing to pay for it? Run a few searches in your niche or genre and see what comes up that is close to your book idea. If everything that pops up is a free guide or a free course and you can't find any books on the subject that are selling, you'll probably need to make some adjustments to your idea to find a market willing to buy your book.

For example, look at this book: *Write Out Loud.* I wanted to write a book that helped authors write their books. I know there is a market for people wanting to write their books (here's looking at you **wink**) and I know they are searching online for tips and advice on how to write their books. However, when you start searching online for *"how to write a book,"* there are hundreds of free guides, articles, free courses, videos, and even podcasts helping people write their books.

That doesn't mean people aren't willing to buy the book, but it does mean the book better do more than just be a simple step-by-step guide on how to write a book. It needs to provide more substance, more information, and a new perspective—it needs to give the reader something that none of the other pieces give them. You can grab basic, regurgitated information for free.

3. What does the competition look like? A lot of authors like to start looking for their comp titles at the same time they start their validation research, but doing that can skew the rest of your research. Some trends and niches are still emerging, in which case, there won't be a lot of complete books out there yet. But these trends are also still so early that there's not a lot of demand for them yet, so if you can get your book out there (remember what I said about being a pioneer) then you'll be in the right place at the right time when that trend takes off.

On the other hand, romance readers are voracious readers—I mean it is *scary* how fast they will read their books. So, you might find a lot of books coming out that might scare you into believing the market is saturated, but they read so many books so fast that they need that many books to come out just to keep up with them.

Determine the size of the market and then determine whether or not their demand is being met. If you find yourself at the beginning of an emerging trend or in a niche that is not having its current demand met, you could break through!

If you find you're behind the trend or that the competition is already providing more than the demand dictates, that doesn't mean your book idea is a bad idea or that you should necessarily stop working on your book idea. Trends come and go, so even though you might be late on the trend now, you could be ready to jump into it later when it comes back around.

And when all else fails, take another look at what *you* can bring to the trend.

Having a Great Book Idea is Not Enough

Doing market research to validate your book idea is an important step, but it's not the only factor that will determine if your book sells. Books don't sell based on ideas.

For example, let's take the premise "an orphan girl is mistakenly given over to be adopted by a family who doesn't want her. All she wants to do is win over their hearts, and finally have a home, but others in town are determined to run her out due to her status as an orphan."

Anne of Green Gables, right? Or is that *Little Orphan Annie? Pollyanna?*

Or how about this one: learn how to stop self-sabotaging your goals so you can get out there and reach your dreams.

Easy right, that's clearly *Fearless* by Rebecca Minkoff, right? Or maybe it's *Year of Yes* by Shonda Rhimes? *Believe It* by Jamie Kern Lima?

Even with an amazing premise, validating a book idea is challenging because there are so many other factors that will determine whether or not the book is a success.

Each of the books I listed is unique and special and amazing in its own way. You've probably got memories of each one. But it's not the premise or the idea that made them special. The premise is just the beginning.

So, if you find yourself staring at a book idea with no discernable market or demand (*yet*), there is still room for you to add in a unique twist and perspective so you can carve out your market yourself.

You May Not Even Need a Market

After all this talk about validating your book idea and trying to determine just how big your market will be to predict sales and success, I also want to make sure you know that *none of this is required*. I am a firm believer that *every* book has its market. Every book has that group of fans out there that will absolutely fall in love with and adore it.

You just have to find them.

Just think for a minute of all the great stories we have around us that were categorized as "failures" and yet despite how abysmal their paperback reception by the critics were at the time, their cult fandoms were so dedicated that they were adapted into some of the most successful movies of all time:

- Fight Club
- Fear and Loathing in Las Vegas
- 1984
- The Hitchhiker's Guide to the Galaxy
- American Psycho

So, if you ask me whether or not you should give up on a story idea when you can't seem to validate it, guess what I'm going to say?

Never censor your ideas.

Planning, Pantsing, or Some P in Between

Some authors are what we refer to as Planners. These are the authors who plan everything out before they even write the first sentence of their book. And they don't stop at outlining their book: they plan out every plot twist, every character, and every setting…they research everything they need to know as much as they can, then they sit down and bang out their book quickly and efficiently.

Other authors are what we call Pantsers. These authors are the ones all your writing memes are based on: the ones who never seem to know what their characters are trying to do and don't understand where the book is going or how it got there. They basically write everything freestyle and see where their story takes them—discovering the plot along the way.

And then there are the authors in between, the ones we call the Plantsers. That's where I fall on the spectrum.

I enjoy the flexibility and therapeutic effect of freestyle writing and seeing where the story takes me, but I need to know the major milestones that I am trying to reach if I want to make sure the book includes everything that I am aiming for and that it follows a coherent path. Having those milestones also helps me structure my writing routine in a way that works with my ADHD (which I will talk about a little bit later).

None of these practices is better than the others. Pantsing isn't more creative than Planning, Planning isn't more thought-out. In fact, most of the time, you can't even tell which way the author wrote their book when you're reading it after the fact. And while I did say that Planners are able to bang out their books quickly and efficiently, that doesn't mean that they are any faster or more efficient than Plantsers or Pantsers.

Let's take a look at a popular quote on planning and productivity to show you what I mean:

Give me six hours to chop down a tree and I will spend the first four sharpening the axe. ~Attributed to Abraham Lincoln

There are several variations of this quote out there, and no evidence that Abraham Lincoln ever actually said it, but all the same, I love this quote. A lot of neurotypical analysts will say that this quote epitomizes the importance of planning and preparation: frontload the work with planning and preparation and you can cut the tree down in just two hours instead of swinging that ax around for six hours.

Sure, on paper that makes sense. But Pantsers, those who hit the ground running with little to no planning, can still finish the book in six hours. They might be swinging the axe the entire time, they might be more tired and might run the risk of hurting themselves, but in the end, they still get the tree down.

And there's the other side of this I'd like you to explore, too…It takes roughly 15 minutes to sharpen an ax today with a sharpening stone and file; I don't know how long it took back in the 1850s to 1860s, but I have to believe that because the tools were somewhat similar to the tools people use today that it would take about the same amount of time. So, if it takes 15-20 minutes to sharpen an ax, why would someone need to spend *four hours* sharpening their ax?

It could be a misquote—like I said there's no actual evidence that he ever said this. But it could also be referencing the amount of overthinking that some of us do when it comes to certain tasks. And if you're overthinking the tasks for the first four hours to the point of procrastinating finishing the actual task, are you really being any more efficient? Or are you just drawing out the task for as long as possible?

The important thing to do here is to *write*. As we're going to discuss in the next chapter, your top priority should be to get that book written the best way you know how.

By the way, if you're wondering where on the spectrum of Ps you fall, you can take this quiz to see: are you a Planner, a Pantser, or are you some P in between by scanning the QR code below:

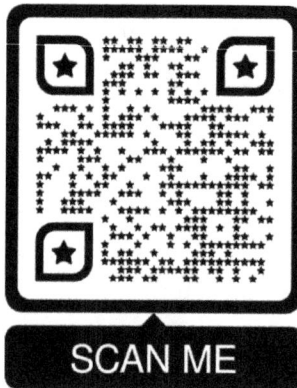

SCAN ME

Research and Your Creativity Cup

Now that you are feeling a little more prepared to start writing your book, let's talk about gathering the materials that you need in order to actually start writing your book.

Even if you are a Pantser, there is going to be at least some level of research that you need to do in order to write your book. You might need to do some historical research to put together a timeline of events or to learn about the subject of your writing. You might want to do some geographical research to learn more about the overall setting where you plan on placing your book.

The good news is that the Internet has placed most of this type of information right at your fingertips, or (even better) in your back pocket on your phone. So, you no longer have to set aside an entire day to go into a library with a notebook and check out half of the bookshelves on a particular event in order to gather the information that you want to write your book. Research today is faster, easier, and much more streamlined than it was when I first started. Which means you can be much more flexible about how and when you do your research.

If you are a Planner, you're probably still going to want to gather your research materials ahead of time. One thing to keep in mind is that it's really easy to get stuck into a procrastination spiral while you are planning, and you may find that instead of making progress that you are getting trapped in this notion of having to become an expert or having to know everything before you can sit down and start writing. This is not the case, and, as I said, research today is much more flexible. So, the biggest thing that you're going to want to research is references and resources.

For example, if I were writing a novel about Jack the Ripper, I would want to know some of the obvious things, such as the names of his victims, the names of the streets where they were found, the names of the people who found the victims, all of the constables who were involved in the investigation, as well as the overall timeline of events. There is no way that I would ever be able to remember all of it. Back in my library days, this would mean writing out a list of the things I needed to know, blocking off at least a day to spend in the library, showing up with my list, talking to the librarian about where I could find some of these answers, and then spending hours going through some of the many books on the subject to jot down the notes from some while also choosing to check out many of the others.

And of course, for the books that I chose to check out and take home with me, there was added time for reading or re-reading entire sections and more notetaking as I tried to build my understanding of that timeline

Today, it's much more efficient for me to hit the internet with an understanding of what I need to know, find the websites that give me that information, and then save them in a spot where I can easily access them whenever I need them. And, as an added bonus, most of the websites that would give me this information contain citations from books that I probably would've found at the library back in the day. So, if I really want to, I can either go to the library with a specific list of books that I want or I can hit up an online bookstore like Amazon to order a book (provided it's a book I think I want to keep on my bookshelf at home, whether for reference or entertainment).

And because you have these sites saved somewhere, you are not beholden to having a full and complete understanding of your subject before you start writing. You can break up the research as needed.

And this goes for Pantsers as well. You might be writing just another werewolf novel and not really thinking about Jack the Ripper until one of your victims stumbles into Whitechapel—and the next thing you know, you're wondering whether or not Jack the Ripper is involved in your novel even as a side character. Or you're wondering if the dialogue that you placed fits with the overall period in which your story is taking place. Either way, you're going to need to do some research in order to fully flesh out the scene and what it means for your book.

While I'm prattling on about research, let's talk about its *other* benefit. Oh yes, research does more than just allow you to find information that will help you write your book. Research can also help you refill your Creativity Cup.

You might be wondering why I would include the Creativity Cup in a section that is supposed to be focused on research…that's because creative research is just as important to your story development as your information research is.

One of the biggest shifts authors go through once they start writing is the shift from *reader* to *writer*. A lot of people think that all writers are readers. This makes sense when you consider that most authors got into writing because of their love of reading and storytelling. Unfortunately, once they start writing, they never really approach reading the same way ever again.

Dun dun *duuuuuunnnnn...*

Instead of allowing themselves to read as they always loved, a lot of authors turn away from reading in their favorite genres, especially if they are writing in those genres, because they develop this fear of their stories being too similar or that they will accidentally plagiarize the other book. But doing this actually robs your brain of the much-needed inspiration that you used to receive back when you were reading in those genres!

Back to the werewolf in Whitechapel idea...if this were a novel I was working on at the moment, you could pretty much guarantee that whenever I wasn't actively researching and writing my book, I would be sitting and streaming nearly every werewolf movie available or reading every werewolf book I could get my hands on:

1. Taking in these other stories with similar concepts helps me stay in an inspired state of mind about the topic at hand in a way that other genres wouldn't be able to do for me. Sure, I could watch Dracula movies instead, but those would just inspire me to write about vampires...not necessarily werewolves. We'll talk about this a little bit later as well.
2. This would also allow me to dissect these stories: what makes them work? What parts don't work? Which themes were prevalent in the movies coming out decades ago that are still prevalent today?
3. And this gives me a chance to dive into my story even deeper: how can I make my story stand out from these other stories? How can I make my story better than this movie? What can I add that hasn't been tried before?

Being able to dig into your inspiration this way helps make sure that you stay there. It helps keep you in the mindset of the story you're working on and allows you to, at the same time, see how you can make your story better.

I don't know about you, but watching a romantic comedy movie doesn't keep me inspired to write a historical paranormal novel. It would just inspire me to write a romantic comedy! Just as like watching *Supernatural* always inspired me to write about paranormal adventures.

And this works for nonfiction as well: watching a cooking show won't inspire me to write a book on personal development—it will just inspire me to write my own cookbook (or, seeing as how I have exactly six recipes, maybe just inspire me to go cook and not write about it at all).

So, while you're researching your book or gathering your resources together, don't forget to build in time to do this creative research as well. Not only will it ensure that your creativity cup stays filled and your inspiration stays top of mind, but it will keep you in the mindset you need for writing the book you want.

Developing Your Characters

Character development is the process of creating relatable characters through which your readers will experience your story. But there's more to developing a great character than slapping a name onto a pronoun and giving them a few lines of dialogue.

10 Steps for Character Development

1. Introduce your character by name as early in the book as you can. Ultimately, your reader needs to be able to connect with your main character, or your protagonist, right away. For your reader to care about any of the other characters in your book, they also need to see how the main character connects to those characters. Why does the main character care about them so much and why should we do the same?

Additionally, when other characters are thrown into a book seemingly out of the blue without a proper introduction, it can confuse the reader. If a new character pops up and appears to take on an important role in the story but hasn't been introduced, a lot of times readers will stop reading in order to go back and see if they've missed anything—which is definitely not a reaction we want readers to have whenever they meet a new character. Surprises are great and fun, but the reader should still be able to follow along with what's happening and with whom.

2. Describe your character to your readers using all five senses. Authors tend to put a lot of thought into how their characters look, but then they leave out some of the other important descriptions that readers will rely on to get a full and clear picture of that character. What does their voice sound like? Is there a popping sound when they speak certain letters? What perfume or cologne are they wearing? Are their hands rough or smooth? What kinds of foods do they like to eat and why? Do they prefer salty or sweet snacks?

Not only will these descriptions help the reader draw up a fuller picture of the character, but this will also keep you from having to constantly add these descriptors throughout your book. I was editing a book for a client a few years ago and every time the main character spoke, she "said softly." When I asked that client for clarification like if this character was whispering, she said that her voice was a naturally soft, raspy voice that rarely rose above a whisper. So, we changed her description near the beginning of the book to include that of her voice and we were able to save a lot of the repetition of "spoke softly" throughout the rest of that series without robbing readers of the ability to hear her.

An important note about your character's descriptions: you don't always have to be as detailed as you might think. There is a growing movement wherein authors will purposely keep the descriptions of their characters vague, allowing their readers to fill in the blanks with their own imagination. This is also fine to do and works very well. In these cases, you will rely more on context and subtext to let your readers know how the characters see themselves, and your readers will draw their own conclusions. As long as you don't put anything into your story that outright conflicts with their image, you'll do fine.

3. **Develop your character's backstory and history as completely as possible.** Think about some of your best friends and how you talk about them to a crowd when they aren't around: how do they come up in the conversation? Bit by bit, you bring up the pieces you know are relevant to that specific conversation at that time. You can do this because you know everything about your best friend already: you know what they're scared of, what they're trying to accomplish, what they've already tried, and what silly dangerous risk they took back in middle school that almost landed them in the hospital.

Talking about your characters should work in the same way, bringing in the relevant pieces of information bit by bit. One of the reasons authors struggle with their characters is that they are also just trying to get to know them. And this is usually when you find large info-dumps in your manuscript that take away from the story or you find a character that seems to fall flat and really doesn't have a defined place within the story.

If you're a Planner, then the easy solution is to brainstorm, develop, and info-dump your characters before you start writing. This way you'll know exactly when to introduce which feature without adding an info-dump. If you're a Pantser, I say go ahead and info-dump away while you're writing. If you're feeling especially industrious, you can always open up a second document to add your character-dump into there as you work. After you feel you've gotten to know your character, this will make introducing those important traits at the right times much easier as you write the rest of your story and help you track these traits as you go. And you can always fix those info-dumps later on in editing.

4. **Develop your character's complete personality and what that adds to the story.** I already talked a bit about your character's description, this time I'm talking about their full personality: how do they handle stress? How do they see the world? Are they generally an optimist, a pessimist, or somewhere in between? What does this personality add to the story? What gap does it fill among the other personalities already present in the story?

This is where you can really get into the psychographics of your character and determine the emotional connection that your reader will have with each character.

5. Develop their flaws of passion. How many times have you heard a reader complain about a character who didn't have any flaws? As we all know, there is no such thing as a perfect person with no flaws (and no, being "too perfect" does not count as a flaw… although being too full of themselves to take advice or direction might be). As human beings, we tend to love too much, hang on for too long, ignore sound advice in favor of following our hearts, take on too much responsibility instead of sharing the burden, and stay quiet when we should be sharing more…there are a lot of traits that we have that when taken to the extreme become a flaw to our character that holds us back, or worse, hurts someone we love.

Our characters are the same way—even if they are aliens from another planet or magical beings dreamt up from another world. They have desires and passions that drive them a certain way and when those passions are taken too far, they and the group as a whole can get hurt. So, think about what flaw of passion your character has and how that flaw affects their relationship with the rest of the characters and the storyline.

6. Give your character a personal objective. One of the biggest mistakes I have seen authors make is forgetting that every character has their own personal objective in any story. This is a pretty easy mistake to make—after all, if your character is part of a group that is trying to save the world from an alien invasion or if they are trying to lead an uprising to overthrow a tyrannical government or bring back civilization—those are both pretty big goals. Shouldn't they be enough?

No, they're not enough.

It's not enough because these are not goals that readers can relate to. Sure, your reader will want to see the bad guys lose. Your reader will want to see the tyrannical government fall, and your readers will want to see the aliens get chased out of the atmosphere. But they can't relate to the motivation and ambition that it takes to carry out that goal.

What they can relate to is trying to prove their parents wrong, trying to win back the love of their life, and trying to make their kids proud. Most readers can't relate to the feeling of climbing Mount Everest, but they can relate to going to the supermarket.

In addition to this, human nature itself tends to be pretty passive when it comes to circumstances outside of our field of vision. The people who want to overthrow that tyrannical government are the people who are the most affected by the tyranny of that government and have a vision of what life might be like without it. The people on the outskirts, where the tyranny has become more ingrained into their daily lives rather than outbursts of terror? They are not as apt to wake up one day and decide it's time for a change, not until a reason comes knocking on their door. And that reason needs to be something personal.

Think about it: we live in a world right now where there is chaos, turmoil, conflict, and war happening all around us. What would have to happen for you to decide to leave your home to go fight all that to make a better world?

That is the level of personal motivation that should be driving your character.

7. **Give your readers access to your character's internal conflicts and struggles.** Every book is going to contain multiple conflicts—it's built right into the premise of the book: the opponent and the disaster. But the internal conflict, that is the battle raging within a character's mind, is where most of the action is actually taking place. This is where characters are striving to better themselves, second-guessing themselves, and doing all that overthinking that the rest of us do on a regular basis.

It can be difficult to really convey what a character is thinking or struggling with internally to the reader, especially if you are writing in the first-person perspective. But think about some of those call signs that tell you when someone is struggling to make a decision or is upset about something. The way that their eyebrows twitch, they might be talking to themselves, they might start scribbling down a list of pros and cons, they might stand at a fork in the road and kick it the dirt before grunting and turning right. Any of these signs can help the reader see deeper into the internal struggle within that character and gives you a way to start drawing it out.

8. Draw on your own experience or on the experiences of people you know to help fill in the gaps as needed. If you're writing fiction, then there is a good possibility that your main character is going to be based heavily on you, especially if this is your first book. They might have your physical traits, pieces of your personality, or they might have characteristics you wish you had, or that you think you would have in a certain situation. It's okay, this happens all the time and it's not bad or self-centered at all. In fact, it can be helpful. Think about how some of your characteristics came about, why some of your perspectives formed, and how they help you see the world.

Then take this concept one step further for the rest of the characters. If you are writing about someone of a different gender, who do you know in real life, that is that gender you could draw inspiration from? Or who is a character on a television show, any television show, that is a member of that gender you could draw inspiration from? What character traits and personalities do they use to survive the world?

9. Show, don't tell. I'm going to fix this just a little bit—show don't tell, is one of the most common pieces of advice you will find out there. It comes from this idea of helping the reader become immersed within the story by doing more than just explaining to them what happens by *describing* what happens in a way that they can experience it. As Anton Chekov said, *"don't tell me the moon is shining; show me the glint of light on broken glass."* This can apply to your characters as well.

Instead of telling your readers that your character is angry, talk about how the rage is boiling up in their chest, how their hand is clenching into a fist, and how their heart is starting to beat faster.

What you don't want to do is to move over to where your book is all showing and no telling—that will make for a very slow book. So, use this strategically to help your readers experience what it's like to be with your character, but not to the point where events that should feel like they are happening quickly, such as a fight, instead drag on for pages and pages.

Show, don't *just* tell.

10. Don't forget to do your research. Even if you are writing a character based on you, chances are that character is going to be experiencing things you haven't experienced yet, which will put them into situations you haven't been in yet. Some of these situations might be dangerous or traumatizing, and some of these situations might be empowering or uplifting. Either way, if it's not something you have intimate knowledge of, you will want to do your research to help fill in the gap between your experience and what you're writing.

For example, I've had several clients who wrote in a scene in which their character experiences sexual-harassment, but they themselves never experienced sexual-harassment. So, we had to work carefully to craft their characters' reactions, both internal and external, in a way that felt authentic to the character as well as believable to the reader. For these clients, it meant talking to some people who had experienced sexual harassment, hearing their story, finding out what it was like in the moment, as well as what it was like for them afterward, what the impact was, and things of that nature. I was also able to help these clients by leaning in on my own experience combined with these answers to come up with the perfect story elements and help them tell the story.

Many authors put their characters through situations that they hope no one would ever have to go through. Unfortunately, millions of people have already gone through these experiences or similar, and so making light of them or glossing over them when you want to use them as a plot device can be harmful to your community and detract from your book. So, it's an important part of character development to understand the limits of your knowledge and find creative ways, through either book research, creative research, hiring a developmental editor or a ghostwriter, or interviews with other people to fill in those gaps and develop your character as responsibly and respectfully as you can.

Character Development for Memoirs and Nonfiction Books

I bet you thought that character development was something only fiction authors had to worry about, but that's not quite true.

Whether you are writing a guide designed to help your readers follow in your footsteps, a personal development book, a self-help book, or even a memoir based on your life, you still need to take a moment and think about the character in your book. On the surface, this looks like an easy answer: obviously, the character in the book is you. And you are half right.

In most nonfiction books, the main character in the book is actually a shared space between you and your reader. Depending on the overall structure of the book and how you decide to tell your story, the front half of the book focuses primarily on your journey up to a certain point, most likely mirroring what the reader is currently experiencing, and the second part of the book becomes your most recent journey from finding the solution forward, which is where the reader wants to go. This means you have to take extra care to ensure that through that first part of the book, your reader is able to relate to you enough to see themselves in your story.

If your reader can see themselves inside your story, understand where your decisions were coming from, understand the choices that were put in front of you, and nod along with your journey, they will be more likely to see themselves following along with you through the second part of that book. They will be more likely to implement your solution, your information, your guidance, and ultimately get to the transformation that you set out to provide them. However, if you simply string together a chronological series of events or things that happened to you, there's no depth or relation to your character. They have no reason to connect with you simply because something happened to you.

You can think of this almost as being trauma-bonded to your reader. They are currently going through that scene you went through a couple of years ago before you started writing your book. They need to see the human side of whatever that part of the story was. And that is where understanding character development comes into play.

Understanding your own emotions and personality traits and the impact they had on your choices through life is going to be crucial to giving your character depth and helping your reader find their place in your book. Showing your flaws of passion, a bit of your backstory, and giving your readers access to your internal conflict throughout your story is going to be integral to the success of your book.

Another thing you want to be mindful of as you are writing your non-fiction book is the concept of show, don't just tell.

If you are writing a book on building a business, and it includes a decision regarding why one business is better for you than the next, you don't want to simply write in *"but the second business was better for me, I just knew it."* That statement is not compelling. How did you know? Were there signs that you spotted? Was it a feeling in your gut, did your excitement grow every time you thought about it, were you able to sit down and brainstorm pages and pages of your plan versus struggling to get started with the other plan? Did your eyes light up whenever someone asked you about it?

These types of physical reactions to our decisions impact how well your reader is able to relate to you and how well they are able to insert themselves at the right time to be that main character and follow along with your journey.

Character Development for Planners

As a Planner, you're going to want to try to develop as many of your characters as possible before you start writing the book. How you want to do this is going to be completely up to you, but I recommend that you choose a place that is readily available next to your document. If you are using a complete writing suite, such as Scrivener, where you can keep your research together in the same file as your manuscript, that's perfect. If you're using a free program, like Google Docs (which happens to be my favorite) then you may want to do your character development in a separate file, but in the same folder. I would even recommend linking your manuscript directly to that character's document just for ease of access while you're writing.

There are several tools and websites that will help you develop a strong character for your book. I also offer worksheets for character development that you are free to grab by scanning the QR code on this page. This can help ensure that you have your character fully planned and written out and all you have to do is make sure you keep the pages stored in your writing space so that you can grab them at any time while you're writing.

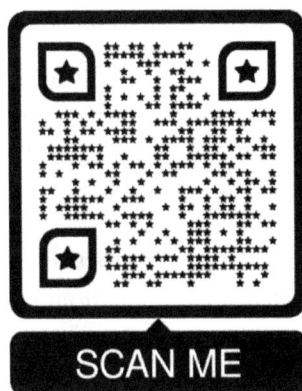

SCAN ME

As with planning some of the other elements of your book, don't get sucked down the rabbit hole of thinking that you have to have it all figured out before you can start writing. Get as much planned as you need to get started; if you've missed anything you can always go back in and add that trait to these profiles after you've started writing.

Character Development for Pantsers and Plantsers

Character development is not something that you do when you are planning your novel and that's it. Pantsers and Plantsers both develop their characters just as thoroughly as Planners do, they just have a tendency to do so on the fly before they realize they need a character. For example, they might have their main character step into a shop, and without realizing it, they now have a love interest they need to put a name on and develop into an actual character.

But Pantsers don't usually stop writing in order to do the same level of character planning, so they develop the character as they go in much the same way they develop their plots.

All the same tips, worksheets, and files that Planners use for their character development work for Pantsers and Plantsers. The only difference is in how you use them.

Instead of filling them all out ahead of your writing, you're going to fill them out as your character divulges their secrets to you in the story. If you discover your character has brown hair, jot it down in the profile. If you later find they walk with a limp favoring their left leg, jot that down. Because you can fill these worksheets and profiles out as you go, you never have to worry about having everything developed all at once and you'll still be able to keep track of those important details.

As far as tracking these traits, for Pantsers I recommend a combination approach: print out a few character profile sheets like the ones I linked above so they are right there in your writing space; as you're writing, pause just long enough to scribble down an important detail on the sheet. After your writing session, you can then also add these details to a digital file online somewhere, so you'll also have them available there.

Write and
Never Look Back

Write and Never Look Back

You might not feel like it yet, but you're ready to start writing. Really!

And this might seem like a silly thing to try to reassure you about this far into this book, but I've had so many new authors ask me about this exact thing: "how will I know when I'm ready to start writing a book? How do I start writing a book??"

So, this is me telling you that you're ready *now*. Whether you've read everything up to this point or you skipped all those front chapters to get to this page: you're ready to start writing.

The good news is that writing the book can really be done in two steps:

1. Write the book
2. Make it good

And they absolutely must be done in that order.

I've lost count of the number of authors who have said something about how much they hate their writing while they're writing. There is a seemingly infinite number of memes and posts online in which authors confess that they can't seem to do their story justice, that everything they write turns to crap, or that they're questioning whether or not they have what it takes to even write a book at all because they seem to be so bad at finding the words they want.

The hardest part about writing a book is figuring out the best way to do it. And this is made harder because whenever you ask another author what the best way to write a book is, they're going to tell you different answers. Writing a book is a personal journey—one that varies from author to author. The strategy that works for one won't work for *every*one. You hear every tip from "*write every day*" to "*write once a week*" to "*write sitting at a computer*" to "*write in bed…get up early, stay up late, fit writing in between other activities and block off hours of time to dedicate to writing.*"

You're probably going to experiment a bit as you try to figure out the best way for *you* to write your book, especially if this is your first book. What matters is that you build a writing routine that works best for you no matter what that looks like.

They Call it a Rough Draft for a Reason

When I was a little girl, I wanted to be an artist so badly. Every year on my birthday, I would get at least two to three of those sketchbooks with the step-by-step illustration examples. You know the ones that start with an oval, and then you draw a sort of cross over the oval to set up the face before you start filling in the shape of the eye and ending with the shading of the nose. Writing is the same process. Artists don't hit the paper shading in hair, they hit the paper by sketching out their base. Sure, some of the more experienced artists might be able to skip a few steps, they might be able to make a cleaner illustration just as experienced authors who have received feedback on their work can often create a cleaner manuscript. But they don't skip their base.

So, let's just get one thing clear right now: get perfection out of your head while you're writing. Writing is not the time to be obsessing over every detail or to be trying to turn out the perfect book. Writing is the time to get your story out of your head and into words that can be edited and shared later.

Step one: write the book.

And chances are, especially if this is your first book, you are hopeful of the high quality you are going to write. You probably have a very high standard, you are expecting great words with very few misspellings, and mastery over punctuation and grammar. There is nothing wrong with striving for excellence. After all, this book will become a part of your legacy, your gift to the world. This book is going to be just one of the many ways that you can leave your mark and impact future generations. Of course it should be excellent.

It just doesn't have to come out of your brain already in excellent form.

When it comes to publishing, books never go directly from the writer's keyboard straight onto a bookshelf. There is an entire process with separate industries dedicated to turning that story into a book available for sale to the masses. There are editors, proofreaders, formatters, as well as publishers. And each one of these industries has its own measure of excellence that they bring to your book. You can't publish a book by skipping any of these steps.

So, get the story out of your head. Write your story in the best words you have, the best way you know how, and get it onto paper. Once you do that, the sky's the limit. Once the story is actually in a file, all of the feedback, editing, formatting and all of those steps that make it look like the excellent book that's in your head can be done. However, trying to do all of those steps at the same time will end up overwhelming and frustrating you and halting your progress on the book.

Your rough draft is your base. This is you throwing sand in the sandbox, downloading all of your ideas on paper, and reciting your story to yourself. And when you're done, you're going to go back through and start shaping it, forming the sandcastles, sharpening your ideas, and revising your story into a can't-put-it-down-page-turner book.

The Trick to Getting Started

Okay, so now you have your ideas flowing, you understand that you are not aiming for a perfect draft, you're ready to get that rough draft on paper… so you sit down at your desk, you open up that word file, and there it is: the dreaded and blinking cursor.

When I first started writing, I truly believed that the reason it was called a *cursor* was because it was a curse. If you get hung up on staring at that blinking cursor on the blank page, it can stop you before you even had a chance to get started.

There is something personal about the anxiety that a blinking cursor brings—no two authors experience it the same way. For some authors, that's the moment that this is all becoming real, and they realize that they are transitioning from whatever it was that they were calling themselves before into an *Author*. And that brings all sorts of images to mind, depending on what it is, they think of when they think of an author. For others, it's a sudden understanding that once they start, they could fail. That blinking cursor represents the green light. Up until that point, writing a book was a dream that could happen. But once you see that blinking cursor, you know it is going to start and you don't know if it's going to finish or if it's going to be successful.

And for others, there is a fear of doing it right. We understand that the first chapter of any book is the most important chapter because that's what sells the rest of the book. And the first line of that first chapter is the most important line because that's the line that is going to help a reader determine how far into the chapter they're going to get. That's a big burden to place on those first few words.

So, let's remove the burden. The first few words of your *finished book* are the most important words of your book. The first few words that you start typing right now *are not* the most important words.

The Trick

To Start Writing Is
To Sit Down And
Start Writing

Remember what I said, you are a better writer than you think you are. Right now, you are just trying to shovel words onto the paper. Everything is going to be revised and refined as you go through the editing process later. For now, just start and get that base going. You will find the perfect opening sentence later down the road.

So, as trite as this sounds, as oversimplified as this sounds, the trick to getting started with writing your book is to sit down and start writing your book. You will discover everything else as you go: the best time of day to write, the best tools to use, the best routine to keep you motivated, and even your voice. Start writing, and as you discover tools or tricks or schedules that work better for you, adopt them into your routine and pivot. As you discover your voice, adjust your writing to include it. Just as with planning your book or developing your characters, you don't have to have everything figured out before you start writing.

You just have to start writing.

Your Anxiety is Lying to You, you are not a Burden

I will never forget the first time I asked my spouse for extra support around the house while I was writing a book. I had just graduated with my master's degree in psychotherapy, our daughter was 18 months old, I had just published my book, *Everything I Need to Know About Parenting I Learned from Watching Star Trek*, with more works in progress on the wings, and I was working on two other books for clients when I started feeling overwhelmed by everything that was happening. He had come home from work and was upset to see that the house wasn't as clean as he wanted it to be, and he was trying to figure out why, if I worked from home, couldn't I get all of these things done?

And I told him that I needed help.

That launched an argument about the kind of help that I needed. I told him I needed someone to come and help me keep up with the laundry and the dishes, I needed help watching our daughter for a few hours out of the day, just basically keeping up with household responsibilities. And he looked me straight in the eye and said that if I couldn't keep the house clean and take care of our daughter on my own, then I probably didn't deserve her.

As you can imagine, this sent me into a spiral that lasted for years. Even after we got divorced, every time I thought of hiring someone to come in and help me catch up on the laundry or spot clean parts of the house, his voice is ringing in my head that I don't deserve the things I have if I am not the one who's taking care of them.

Let me pause here to let you know that if you are having similar thoughts, *they could not be further from the truth.*

Every time I start on a new book, I get so excited over the book and over the subject matter that I end up sitting at my computer for hours and hours during the first few days, from the minute I wake up until well into the night. Sometimes I don't even realize that I haven't even eaten until after my kids come up to me asking for a snack.

There's just something about this rush of excitement and inspiration whenever you're writing a book that takes over everything. And you want to grab hold of that motivation while you're still excited and use it to the best of your ability to get as much written and out of your head as possible before you could lose momentum or lose your idea altogether.

Unfortunately, sometimes all of this extra writing comes at the expense of other things. Things get piled up. And sometimes, responsibility shifts.

Now, I realize it does not have to happen this way. You can absolutely decide to wake up early in order to work on your book before anyone else wakes up, you can relegate your writing time to only your spare time on the weekends to make sure that nothing else falls by the wayside. There are plenty of authors out there who are able to steadily write their books using their spare time, a few minutes here or there, and they continue to plug away at their book for months or years to get it done.

But most authors don't have "spare time" and even if they did, they don't want to take years to write their books. Most of the authors I've met wish they could get their book written in a month or two months, certainly under the one-year mark. And for these authors, that usually means being able to set aside their other responsibilities, at least for a time, so they can focus on writing their book. This might mean letting some of their household chores decline, or it might mean allowing some of the responsibility to shift over to a partner or older children, or even hiring someone to come in and take care of these household chores for you.

Unfortunately, a lot of my clients who went this latter route ended up feeling guilty for allowing parts of their household to go by the wayside, or for having to have their spouse or family take over certain responsibilities. And a lot of them struggled to justify paying money to hire someone to come in and take care of these things for them when their book hadn't even been published yet, much less selling and bringing in any money. I have struggled with a lot og that same guilt. The important thing to remember with whatever decision you make here is that *you are making the best decision for you and your book.*

If you know that the best way for you to get your book finished is to be able to put all of your focus into that book for a short time, then that's what you need to do. The alternative is to either never start writing your book at all, and always feel a sense of unfulfilled guilt for never having started your book, or actually being able to start writing your book, but not being able to finish it, leaving you with a very real feeling of failure for not being able to make the commitment you needed to be able to make to finish your book.

On the other hand, if you know the only way you can finish your book is to consistently plug away at it whenever you could without pulling too much of your attention away from other responsibilities, then whenever you sit down to write for too long, that feeling of guilt for ignoring your other responsibilities will end up eating at you and distracting you from being able to write at all when you do half the time.

If you have the support of family around you to help you take care of yourself and your business, I want you to remember that this is *family* and that's why they are there. That's what they signed up for when they decided to cultivate a relationship with you, whether it be siblings, partners, or even parents. I know that telling you not to feel guilty for relying on them won't work, so instead, I will remind you that if they are offering to support you, and you need their support, then you are not doing anything wrong by accepting that support.

If you don't have the support of family around you and you need someone to help you take care of yourself and your business, there is still support available. You can find online partners and writing groups, there are writing communities that meet regularly at various libraries and coffee houses. There are virtual assistants, housekeepers, babysitters, YMCA clubs, all available to help you take care of your business, take care of your house, and take care of your children so that you can concentrate on your book. And again, using these services to help you get your book done is not a burden. That's why these services exist, so they can help the people who need the help.

At the very beginning of this book, I said every story matters and *your* story matters. And I meant it. And I believe you deserve every bit of help that comes your way to help you tell your story. If that means finding someone to help you take care of your kids for a couple of hours a week, you deserve it. If that means letting the dishes pile up for a couple of extra days, then let them pile up. It does not make you a bad person to take some of your focus and place it on your book.

And the best piece of advice that I can give you now is to talk to your family before you start writing your book and let them know what it is you want to do. Chances are, if you have family around who are genuinely supportive of you, you have already told them. But now it's time to have a serious discussion with them about what that means as far as temporary changes in availability and the division of responsibilities; what kind of help will you need in order to finish your book? This will help bring everything out into the open before you even start writing, their expectations will be set, and they will be able to reassure you of their commitment to helping you themselves.

Finding the Time to Write

Most new authors don't decide to become authors because they have all this extra time sitting around in their schedule and nothing to fill it with. Nope, most new authors already have other full-time responsibilities; they are business owners or they have a day job or they are students or parents or all of the above. Most new authors have family obligations and many at least try to have a social life with friends. What they don't have is a whole lot of spare time just sitting around.

And that means that most new authors are trying to figure out how they are going to find the time to write their book.

This is especially difficult because no one can tell you how much time it's going to take you to write your book. If you search online for *"how long does it take to write a book"*, you will find dozens of websites telling you that you can write a book a weekend, write a book in ten days, write a book in thirty days, write and publish a book in a year. And if you go into writers' groups and talk to a lot of authors and ask them how long it took them to write a book, you will hear answers along the same lines. I have one client who sat down and was able to write her book in *27 hours*, and I have another client who came to me to edit her book once she finally finished, even though it took her 30 years to finish it.

And that's just the tip of the iceberg. I know some authors who got lulled into a false sense of security because they were able to finish the first book in three months, only to struggle for two years before they finished the second book in the same series. I know other authors who spent three years on their first book but were able to whip their second book out within a matter of weeks.

How can you plan for the time it takes to write a book when you don't know how much time it's going to take to write the book?

Before I had kids, I was staunchly routed on the side of pantsing my way through projects and sitting down to write whenever the mood struck. Being single and childless definitely gave me the privilege of being able to approach my writing in a very unstructured, almost frivolous manner. I didn't have to worry about hours of operation, I didn't have to worry about tracking my time, and if I was in the shower when an idea struck me, I could just jump out and jot my idea down, sit down and start writing.

Back in 2007, I joined my first attempt at NaNoWriMo, a global writing challenge, where authors from around the world come together and each tries to write 50,000 words during National Novel Writing Month. And I started off the month writing just as I normally wrote, whenever the mood struck. Then I found a group running writing sprints, which I had never heard of before this point, and I decided to join in because it looked like a lot of fun. By the end of that month, I had written more words than I had ever written in a single month in the years leading up to NaNoWriMo. And I thought, wow...*I wish I could do this every month.*

So, guess what I did that very next month?

I went right back to my old habits: no planning, at all, just writing whenever the mood struck. I didn't even check into any of the writing groups I had joined during NaNoWriMo. And it went on like this for years:

1. Join NaNoWriMo in November.
2. Do writing sprints.
3. Finish more words in that month than I finished most months.
4. Go back to my old habits in December and forget until the next November.

It wasn't until I was pregnant with my daughter that I realized this was not going to work for me. In fact, it was because I didn't really have other obligations outside of myself that it seemed to work at all. And you have to remember, I was working as a ghostwriter, so writing *was* my job—I wasn't even trying to balance out a day job.

But now, with a husband and a daughter on the way, the inspiration and mood to write never seemed to strike at a time when I could actually sit down and take advantage of it. It always seemed to strike when I had a doctor's appointment or when my back was hurting. And after my daughter was born, it got worse. Then inspiration always seemed to strike when my daughter was crying for food or a diaper change or just to be held. Not to mention my own focus was being pulled in one million different directions, my anxiety was off the charts, and I hadn't fully transitioned into my new identity as a mom yet.

Three weeks later, I decided to sit down and try writing sprints on my own, outside of writing groups and NaNoWriMo…and they absolutely changed my everyday approach to writing. Soon after that, I started the long, often uncomfortable, process of shifting over from Pantser to Planner, landing right in the middle as a Plantser. And my writing career finally started to truly take off from there.

Now, I am not telling you this in order to say that you have to be a Plantser or a Planner in order to be a successful author, just that if you give yourself enough time to really work through some of the various methods out there, and if you reflect on all your strengths as a writer and how you can harness the strengths better, you will find a system and strategy that works for you. From there, putting together the time to write will be much easier because you'll stop fighting how your brain works, stop fighting to squeeze in writing time, and you'll finally see how it all fits together for you.

Using Writing Sprints

So, what are writing sprints and how did they magically fix my career as a writer?

Writing sprints are exactly the way they sound: a fast and focused dash in which you bang out as many words as possible. But it's not quite as easy to just transition into sprints if you haven't trained yourself to use them properly.

Think of writing sprints the same way you think about running, you have your marathon runners who are running 26 miles at a slow and steady pace, and then you have your sprinters who are dashing along the track for a few hundred yards. They are very different types of the same activity and they require very different training and preparation.

If you have never done a writing sprint before, it can be hard to focus your brain in a way that allows you to bang out a lot of words in a short, concentrated amount of time. A lot of first-time sprinters get frustrated with the process because they feel like their brain can't come up with the words fast enough for a sprint. They feel pressured to write or type quickly and then feel anxiety when they can't keep up with themselves and have to pause.

When I made the decision that writing sprints were going to be the primary method for writing any draft, I started with five-minute sprints. With a kitchen timer, I would sit down at my laptop, set the timer for five minutes, and start writing.

Once the timer went off, I would stand up and leave my laptop to go take care of whatever might need my attention: my daughter, the cat, the dog, the dishes, my bladder—anything that was not on my laptop. 25 minutes later, I would return to my laptop, reset the timer for another 5 minutes, and sprint again.

Those first few sprints were *crap*. I barely got over 15 to 20 words out. I was distracted through most of them, focused on how fast I was typing and trying not to sit and think too long but also finding myself in situations where I had to sit and think. What I found was I was still trying to come up with names for characters or cities, and I was still trying to figure out what to do next in my book. And these types of decision points took me out of the writing. And as you probably know, once you're out of the writing, it's hard to get back in. So, my next step was to separate those decision points from the sprints.

I did this by adjusting the break. Instead of spending 25 minutes away from my laptop taking care of other responsibilities, I cut that down to about 15 minutes. Then I would return to my laptop and use the next 10 minutes preparing for my next sprint: looking at what I had just written and figuring out what I wanted to write next. Then, I would start the timer for another 5 minutes and start sprinting again.

These next few sprints were better; I jumped up to about 50 words per sprint, which isn't bad. But now what I noticed was that because I was reading what I had already worked on when I set the timer I wasn't always picking up where I left off. Instead, some of my time was spent fixing or revising parts of what I had just written in the sprint before. So, I adjusted the break again.

Like most authors, I have an impressive collection of notebooks. So, I grabbed one of these notebooks, and for my next sprint, when the timer went off, instead of immediately, leaving my laptop to go take care of other responsibilities for 25 minutes, I spent 1 minute writing out a quick summary of what I had just written about as well as a quick directional statement of what I wanted to write next. After my 15-minute break, when I sat back down at my laptop, instead of re-reading everything I had already written, I looked over that notebook and solidified my plan for the next sprint.

This is when writing sprints *finally* took off for me. By looking at how I was spending my time in and around the sprints and adjusting my breaks, by removing that review, I had learned how to stop my inner editor from creeping up into my writing and could now just focus on getting the words out. This was when I started banging out 150 to 200 words in a 5-minute writing sprint.

After a few weeks, I upped it to 10 minutes, then 15 minutes. As my kids grew and were able to entertain themselves for longer spans before needing me, I tried even longer sprints, I got up to his highest 45-minute sprints with a 15-minute break.

What I found is that the 20/10 sprinting method worked best for me.

1. 20 minutes of concentrated effort on writing.
2. A 10-minute break is split into 1 minute of jotting down my summary and thoughts in a notebook and 9 minutes of taking care of things away from my document.

I usually tell people who are not sprinters by nature to start at that five-minute level with a 25-minute break and see what tweaks help them get better, then start to scale up until they find their sweet spot. 45-minute sprints work incredibly well for a number of authors I've met over the years, but I was not able to get my brain to focus on writing for that long. After about 20 minutes, my focus starts to pull away from my writing, which makes the words slow down.

The real trick for writing sprints to work for you is to be able to continuously write for the full time that the clock is running without stopping to think about things like names or other sticking points that so many authors tend to overthink. My general rule of thumb now is if it takes me longer than 10 seconds to put in a word, use a placeholder. Then, outside of writing sprints, that's when I'm going to go back and figure out the right word for what I was trying to say.

Using Dictation to Write

Five years ago, I could not stand the idea of dictation. I heard so many authors, bloggers, journalists, and other writers singing the accolades of dictation and how much it helped with their productivity and word counts, and yet I could never seem to make it work. It felt as though every time I tried to use it, I was spending more time editing the jumbled mess of letters and text than it would have taken me to simply write out the words during a single sprint.

And it didn't seem to matter what kind of software I used. I had friends telling me that it was because I was buying the cheap software and I needed this other, $300 software in order to make it work because that dictation software would learn my accent which would lessen the need for edits after. And when that didn't work, they told me I didn't have the right microphone, I needed a bigger and better microphone that didn't pick up all the background noise.

Well, that didn't work either.

It wasn't until one of my clients and a fellow NaNoWriMo participant equated using dictation to using their non-dominant hand to write that it clicked and I got it. I was trying to use my nondominant hand to write and expecting my handwriting to just look as it always did. Of course, things don't work like that – the body doesn't work like that. You can learn how to write with your non-dominant hand, and you can even develop very nice handwriting with your non-dominant hand, but it takes months of a concerted effort to do so. Heck, it took years to develop decent handwriting with your dominant hand, so why was I expecting to be able to use dictation to write and have it work exactly the same as using my laptop when I hadn't learned how to dictate?

And yes, there is a finesse to dictation.

So, if you are going to try to use dictation to help you write your book faster, here are a few tips that will help you out.

1. **Practice speaking with clear and strong enunciation.** If the word ends with a T, make sure you pronounce that T. The same with other letters that many English speakers tend to leave off: Rs, Ds, Gs... we all have certain words where some of the letters get dropped, either in the middle of the word or at the end of the word. Dictation software has gotten very good at picking up some of these letters just based on the context of the words you're using around that, but it's not perfect yet. The more clearly you can pronounce these letters, the easier it is to train your dictation software.

2. **Practice speaking while verbalizing your punctuation.** Different dictation software picks up on punctuation differently. Some of them will add in a comma every time you pause, and some of them won't. Most of them will end up with a gigantic, running long sentence if you don't put in your periods and a gigantic paragraph, spanning pages, if you don't put in the line breaks. But these elements are things we insert into our speech without really thinking about it, and our word processors help us insert these things into our writing, so we don't have to concentrate on it. Therefore, when you all of a sudden have to think about whether or not you need a comma in a sentence and saying it out loud so that the dictation software can pick up on it, it feels unnatural.

I can reassure you, however, that it does get easier with practice. In fact, as I was practicing verbalizing my punctuation and getting better at dictation, my kids started picking up the same habits and, sometimes, would even verbalize their own punctuation as they spoke to their friends or other members of the family.

3. Practice your speaking speed. Human beings have wild, speaking patterns. They will speak slowly for one minute, with pauses and filler words as they try to pull out the next words in their thoughts. And when they are passionate about something, they will spill dozens of words between breaths. Unfortunately, the dictation software doesn't pick up on these different speaking habits very easily.

Sometimes the microphone will shut off while it is waiting for you to pull up that thought. Other times it will add in a rogue comma that you did not ask for simply because you paused and it seemed like a natural spot to add in a comma given the context around it. The best way I have been able to work around these things is to practice speaking at a steady pace. Even when I am approaching a subject I am passionate about, something I would normally rant about quickly without having to pause for a breath, I find it easier for the dictation software to pick up my words and punctuation correctly when I slow down my speech, practice my enunciation, and make the words flow steadily rather than in these passionate bursts.

There are a lot of benefits to mastering the art of dictation when you want to write a book. For one thing, even when you are slowing down your speech to practice consistency and enunciation, most of us still speak faster than we type. This means you can get more words out in less time by using dictation. Additionally, dictation allows you to write in a more authentic and conversational manner, which is usually much easier to read than the long words that come out of our fingertips when we are using a computer. It's easier to choose words that roll off the tongue when you're dictating than it is when you're hitting keys on a keyboard. And it also lowers the barrier of access to writing and removes the burden of having to be an excellent speller or master of grammar in order to write a book.

Although, if you ask me, even if you decided not to use dictation and you wanted to use a laptop, there still should not be any burden on you to be an excellent speller or to have a mastery over grammar rules. Like I said before, write your story using the best words you have, and don't worry one bit about whether or not they're spelled correctly. You can always fix them later. Right now, the most important thing is that you get words on the page in any way you can.

Tracking Your Writing Sessions

Regardless of how you find the time to write or how you choose to write, tracking your writing sessions is an invaluable tool for establishing your baseline and for watching your progress over time. Any day that goes by and you haven't made as much progress as you were hoping to make can suddenly make you feel as though you're wasting your time. Go through a few bad days in a row and it's easy to start falling into a spiral.

But tracking your sessions gives you a chance to see how you're doing over time, even around those few bad days in a row.

Most authors judge their progress by the last few writing sessions rather than over time. However, since writing slumps can sometimes last days or even weeks, that means that when you're in one it can be almost impossible to remember the last good writing day you had. Tracking your progress helps you through that. I use a Writing Session Tracker to help me track and recognize my progress as well as reflect on how that session is working and if there is anything I need to work on before my next writing session. This also helps me keep from going back and re-reading my writing too early.

You can use anything you like to track your writing sessions, but I do also have a Writing Session Tracker you can grab by scanning the QR code here:

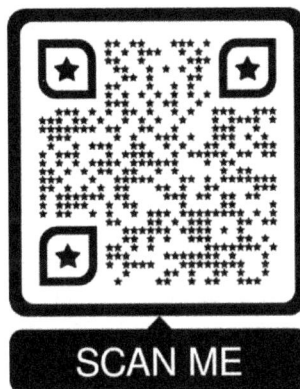

Staying Motivated to Write Every Day

First off, let me start this section by telling you that you do not need to write every day. I hear it all the time: if you want to make money from your writing, then you need to write every day.

I hate this advice so much—not only is it not true, it's ableist and potentially harmful.

What is true is that if you want to make a living writing, then you need to make a consistent effort toward finishing your book. And sometimes that means writing when you don't really feel like it, which leads me to one of the most common questions people ask me: how can you force yourself to write every day?

Before I tell you that, let's talk about your locus of control and how it affects your progress and, more importantly, how it affects the way you look at your progress.

The Locus of Control

Back in 1998, Columbia University did a study about motivation in which they took a large group of fifth graders and assigned them numerous challenging puzzles to work on by themselves. After some time, they went to every participant and told them they did well. For half the participants, they told them they did well because they were so smart, but for the other half of those participants, they told them they did well because they tried so hard.

For the next round of tests, they gave each of these participants three more puzzles of varying difficulty. For the kids who had been praised for being so smart, they spent most of their time tackling the easiest puzzles or no puzzles at all. But for the other half of the participants, those who were told they did well because they had tried so hard, they spent most of their time tackling the more difficult puzzles and refused to give up. At the end of the study, those who had been told they were smart said that they didn't really like the study, while those who were told they worked hard explained that they really did like the study.

What this and other studies like this show is the link between our motivation and where we see our *locus of control*. For the students who were told they were smart, being smart is an external locus of control. Human beings can't control whether or not they are born smart or have access to the libraries and education to make them smart. On the other hand, the students who were told they worked hard had an internal locus of control. While students can't control whether or not they are born smart, they can control how hard they work to find an answer.

You can also see this in book marketing as well. Whenever I meet with a new author to put together a marketing strategy, I always start with the question about what their book sales look like now and why? If they tell me things like nobody reads anymore, nobody's buying books, the time of year that the book was released, or other events happening, then I know that they have an external locus of control. They are assigning nearly all control over their success to forces they could never control, which means it's going to be a more difficult climb for them to reach their goals.

Contrary to this, if that author tells me they didn't have a website set up, they weren't posting on social media consistently, or they weren't using their email list effectively, now I know that author has an internal locus of control. They understand their path to success relies on factors that are within their control. This makes for a much easier conversation as we are putting together a strategy.

And the same thing applies to writing: authors who leave the control over their writing progress in the hands of how distracting or needy their families are or how much their work needed them that week have an external locus of control. But authors who say their progress was small because they took a break or chose to spend more time with family have an internal locus of control.

People who feel like nothing they do matters because something outside of their control will always block them tend to lose motivation quickly. It's very easy for them to burn through their motivation and give up. On the other hand, for people who recognize their own power to influence their success even despite the things that are out of their control, it's much easier for them to stay motivated and keep going because they know they can make a difference.

So, if you have an external locus of control, how can you start moving toward an internal locus of control? And is that even possible?

Of course it's possible! But it starts by praising your progress rather than denouncing it.

I hear authors all the time talking about how they wish they could write 5,000 words in a day or 10,000 words in a day; how they wish they could write 1,000 words in a single writing sprint or how they really want to write, but they just can't seem to do more than 200 words. And my thought is, *are you kidding me?*

200 words is huge! It's a full page. You worked hard for those 200 words; you should be patting yourself on the back for those 200 words. Not punishing yourself because they aren't 1,000 words.

You can't always control when inspiration strikes or when your motivation is at an all-time high. You can't always control when your family needs you or when your kids get sick. But you can make progress all the same. And if you can recognize that progress when it happens, you will feel motivated to keep going.

So, how do I force myself to write every day? I *don't*. I force myself to go through my routine every day and I force myself to recognize my progress *as progress* every day.

Habits will Help You Strike Inspiration

Of course, no matter how good you are at following your routine, inspiration is still going to come and hit you whenever it wants. As Maya Angelo said, "*you can't use up creativity. The more you use, the more you have.*" This is one of the amazing things about being a creative person, that as long as you continue creating, you won't run out of things to create.

But this also means that the more consistently you are writing, the more those ideas are going to come at you at weird times.

And when they do, take the hint.

I come across authors all the time who say something to me like "I would love to write right now, but I have to do the dishes." Can your dishes not wait for an hour?

And don't get me wrong here, I am not advocating for you to completely abandon all of your other chores and responsibilities. But if you find that inspiration and that motivation have struck at the same time, how long before it goes away? Not only that, but sometimes putting that off so you can do this chore you really don't like ends up killing the motivation you had for writing in the first place.

So, if you find yourself in a position where you really want to write, you have the idea, the motivation is welling up within you, but there's just this one chore: you have my permission to put the chore off and go write for 20 minutes or an hour.

You may not be able to do this with everything that pops up: don't stop driving in order to pull over into a rest stop just so you can write for 20 minutes. But we live in a world where we are constantly told that we have to do things we hate before we can do things we love, and that's just not true. Sometimes we have do things we hate, but that doesn't mean that they have to come before the things we love, and it doesn't mean that they have to come *instead* of the things we love. And if we are building a life just doing things we hate because they have to be done, then what kind of life is that?

Writing when Inspiration Strikes Back

Of course, no matter how good you are at following your routine, inspiration is still going to come and hit you whenever it wants. As Maye Angelo said, you can't run out of inspiration; the more you use it, the more you get. This is one of the amazing things about being a creative person, is that as long as you continue creating, you won't run out of things to create. But this also means that the more consistently you are writing, the more those ideas are going to come at you at weird times.

And when they do, take the hint.

I come across authors all the time who say something to me like "I would love to write right now, but I have to do the dishes." Can your dishes not wait for an hour?

And don't get me wrong here, I am not advocating for you to completely abandon all of your other chores and responsibilities. But if you find that inspiration and that motivation have struck at the same time, how long before it goes away? Not only that but sometimes putting that off so you can do this chore you really don't like ends up killing the motivation you had for writing in the first place. So, if you find yourself in a position where you really want to write, you have the idea, the motivation is welling up within you, but there's just this one chore: you can put the chore off and go write for 20 minutes or an hour.

You may not be able to do this with everything that pops up, don't stop driving in order to pull over into a rest stop just so you can write for 20 minutes. But we live in a world where we are constantly told that we have to do things we hate before we can do things we love, and that's just not true. We have to sometimes do things we hate, but that doesn't mean that they have to come before the things we love, and it doesn't mean that they have to come instead of the things we love. And if we are building a life just doing things we hate because they have to be done, then what kind of life is that?

Write Something You're Passionate About

Earlier in this book, I talked about the impact that your story would have on the lives of your readers and how much I believe in that impact. But no matter how good your idea is or how well you know a subject, it is about eleventy-billion times easier to stay motivated to write it if it's a subject you're passionate about.

When you write your first draft, that is for you. The more you love the idea, the more excited you will be to get it onto paper. The more motivated you will be to finish it. If you are writing a romance novel with zombies, and you don't like romance or zombies, you are not going to feel motivated to finish that book. If you are writing a book on how to start a fashion business, and you have no interest in fashion whatsoever, it's going to come through in your draft, if you are even able to finish, which you probably won't be able to.

There are going to be days that you hate your writing, but you should never hate the topic or the premise of your book.

The draft is for you, and the rewrites are for your readers. This is where you will take that story that you are so passionate to share and turn it into something they can be equally passionate to read.

This is where having a purpose for your book can really help you pull through when you hit those days that you were just not feeling it. Think about the reader's experience from your book: are they going to learn something life-changing, are they going to see a representation of themselves, are they going to learn a new skill or build a new business? What kind of an impact can your book have?

I am not trying to imply that every single book has to have a life-altering world-impacting purpose. Your purpose can simply be to give a reader a one-night escape from their hum drum life. However, if you are able to dig up a purpose for your book, you'll find that desire to impact someone else's life in a positive way which can be very motivating.

Your passion for the subject will motivate you to keep writing; uncovering your readers' passion for the subject will motivate you to get through the rest of the process and publish your story.

Writing with ADHD

I have 38 works in progress right now sitting on my computer. And I don't mean series, either. I probably have closer to 80 works in progress if I counted individual books within a series as a separate WIP.

This has always been a source of guilt and shame for me…a reminder that I like to start a lot of projects but then I struggle to get them finished. And I know that there are plenty of authors out there who have dozens of works and progress hanging out in their computer files, scribbled across notebook pages, drafted up somewhere only to collect dust in a corner, instead of ever receiving the care and edits that it needs to become published. But to me, it didn't matter that the other authors were doing this. To me, this collection of works in progress was proof that I struggle to finish things. That I get excited to start a new project and then once that project is moving, progress is being made, and I get a new idea, I get more excited about the new idea, and I chase the new dopamine.

And my other project dies a horribly lonely death in the corner of my backup drive somewhere because I have moved it off of my computer to save room for the next collection of works.

Two years ago, I started to see this as a bit of a paradox. Because while I have 38 works in progress sitting at various stages of completion, I have also ghostwritten 61 books for clients. That's no small accomplishment.

And I have completed projects in my own name as well, including my book, *Everything I Need to Know About Parenting I Learned from Watching Star Trek*, as well as various courses and planners that I have developed and published to help clients and other authors write and publish their books.

So, if it wasn't that I *couldn't* finish projects, what was it?

In 2021, I was diagnosed with ADHD and when I tell you that all of a sudden I could see everything so much clearer: it was like this giant brick wall standing in front of me finally toppled and I could see past it. All of a sudden, so many things in my life made sense.

The next thing I had to do was figure out what kind of an impact my ADHD had on my writing, particularly when it came to finishing projects and why certain projects would lose their charm and others were easier to finish.

It's been 2 years since my diagnosis, and I am by no means an expert in ADHD. In fact, I am still very much learning. But if you have ADHD and you are struggling to write your book, or if you're afraid to start your book because of ADHD, then I want to share with you what I've discovered in these two years and how I have been able to work with my ADHD to get things finished.

Motivation and Rewards with ADHD

The first major difference between the books I have finished for clients and the books I have not finished was the timing of the reward. When I am writing books for my clients, I am often rewarded in two ways: upfront and as I go. Whenever I hit a particular milestone, I get a payday, I get feedback, and I get to hear the client tell me what kind of impact I am having on their book or on their business.

With my own books, the reward doesn't come until after the book is out and has sold an indeterminable number of copies. So, once that initial burst of dopamine from starting a new project wears off, the only dopamine-inducing-reward left keeping me motivated to work on that book is the promise of reward after it's in a bookstore. But as you know, there are a lot of things that have to happen before that book can get into the bookstore, not the least of which is that the book has to be written.

Setting up a series of rewards and a chain helps with this. A chain is created by crossing off a date on a calendar or filling in a box on a daily habit tracker. I get a small but powerful dopamine hit every time I get to add a link onto a chain. And I don't like breaking the chain, so depending on what the chain represents, I'm going to do my best to make sure I get to add that link onto it.

This is actually the process I'm using to make sure that I finish this book here.

This book has been on my radar to write for more than ten years now. I had the first outline set up in 2011. But I did not trust myself to be able to finish it because of the number of unfinished works in progress cluttering my hard drive. But once I was diagnosed with ADHD and I started digging into what that actually meant—how growing up with undiagnosed ADHD affected my life, what things in my life might have been different if I had understood a little bit more about what my brain was lacking and why I always seemed to be fighting against it—I was able to see just how even something like setting up a chain on a habit tracker could make such a tremendous difference.

All this time I thought I was scatterbrained, and it turned out all I needed to do was set up a system where progress in the book was giving me daily dopamine hits and could be added to the chain.

Planning and the Muddy Middle

Another major difference I picked up between the books I was finishing for my clients versus the books I was not finishing for myself was the planning involved. You see, ghostwriting isn't just when a client gives me an idea and I run with it to write a book…ghostwriting is about me writing *their* story. Adopting their voice and experiences to share a book that looks and reads exactly as it would if they'd written it themselves.

My clients and I always planned out their books as part of the adoption phase. Sometimes, my clients came to me with a fully developed outline for me to follow. Other times, the client and I would sit together and develop the outline so we could agree on the content and strategy of the book before I got started.

But when it came to writing my own books, I was trying to pants my way through everything. I was trying to discover the plot and the characters and let things unfold as they will, surprising me along the way. And I really did love the surprise of finding out just how certain things would fit together in the end.

But here is where pantsing actually worked against my ADHD plodding through that muddy middle.

You see, most authors are able to figure out how they want their book to start. And most authors are able to figure out how they want their book to finish. But when it comes to the middle, ideas don't seem to be flowing as much anymore. Motivation starts to wane and you start questioning whether or not your book makes any sense or if there's enough action to keep readers engaged.

By that point, you're so far into the manuscript that you've lost that "new book smell" yet you're so far from being done that you can't start sprinting toward that finish line just yet.

And you feel stuck.

As a Pantser, I was very much a linear writer. That meant I had to write chapter one before I could write chapter two, which I had to finish before I could write chapter three. And this meant that if my book lost my interest, for one reason or another, then just about anything else could come in and grab my interest—including another book idea.

But with my client books being preplanned, I didn't have to finish the boring stuff that was dragging me down in order to get to the next part. Having the plan unlocked my ability to write things out of order. With the plan, if I was stuck in the muddy middle and unsure of how to write chapter seven, I could skip ahead to chapter nine and get that same sense of excitement. Then, once I had the motivation built up and I had that momentum going from making progress on chapter nine, it would usually unlock my ability to figure out chapter seven, which allowed me to go back and fill in the gap.

This was not something I was able to easily translate back to the novels I was pantsing because I didn't know what was coming up in that novel. Without having at least part of the plan laid out, I didn't know what was going to happen further in the book and, therefore, there was nothing in that book that could get me excited the same way.

Focus and Wandering Thoughts

I mentioned earlier when I was talking about research and your creativity cup how beneficial it is to pay attention to the arts around you that are similar to the type of book you are writing. But this is even more important when you have ADHD.

You see, as I was trying to learn what my diagnosis meant and how I could change the way I approach certain processes to work better with my brain, the idea of visual reminders kept coming up. Things like wearing a dust mitten when you're cleaning the house, even if you're not using it to dust, just so that it can visually remind you that you are in cleaning mode should you start to wander. Carrying a tote into a room to fill with things that will be carried out as you are clearing clutter to help you avoid leaving that room and being distracted with whatever happens in the next room.

Have you ever gotten a burst of motivation and decided today was the day you were going to straighten out your bookshelf? So, you start taking things off the bookshelf and re-organizing the books, and then you see a notebook that you had thrown up there. So you decide that you need to put that notebook away, and the best place for it is by your desk. So you take the notebook over to your desk, open up the drawer, and decide that while you're there, now is a good time to go ahead and clean out that drawer to put the rest of your notebooks in. Why the sudden change in focus away from organizing your bookshelf to cleaning out the drawer? Because the visual reminder in your hand was the notebook.

And this can continue even further. Say you grab a pile of paper that needs to get thrown away, so you carry that pile of paper into the kitchen to toss it into the garbage can and notice that there are dishes in the sink. So, while you're in the kitchen anyway, you might as well wash the dishes. Now you are at least three activities away from organizing your bookshelf, which still isn't done yet.

That is exactly what happens when you have ADHD and you forcibly remove art from your life that is related to the book you were trying to write. I realized this was another major difference between the books I was able to finish for my clients and the books that were sitting on my hard drive unfinished.

Part of the process of writing a book for my clients includes interviews with my client to get their stories as well as research on the subject matter at hand. When I am writing a book on how to use Twitter for marketing, I am watching YouTube videos on Twitter, I am reading other books on Twitter, I am reading blog articles on Twitter, and I am interviewing Twitter experts and their employees. And it's the same thing for any platform.

When I was ghostwriting books on psychology, I was interviewing psychologists, I was reading books on psychology. I ghostwrote a memoir on antiracism by doing research on antiracism.

And this goes beyond just research for non-fiction. When I was ghostwriting a series of books on werewolves, I read other books on werewolves because my client wanted a book that mimicked the same emotional response from the reader. I watched werewolf movies, I watched legends and histories of werewolves on YouTube, and I read short stories that had werewolves in them.

On the other hand, when I wanted to write my own book about Jack the Ripper, I stopped reading books about Jack the Ripper. I stopped watching YouTube videos and movies that had Jack the Ripper. And because my Jack the Ripper book was slated to contain vampires, I stopped watching vampire movies. I stopped watching YouTube videos about vampires.

In my head, I was protecting my story from the possibility that I might accidentally plagiarize another author's work—which is something I know so many other authors do as well. But what I was really doing was removing the visual reminders my brain needed to stay on task. By watching a documentary on the Triangle Shirtwaist Factory Fire, I was inspired to start writing a novel about that. Then I stopped watching anything about the Triangle Shirtwaist Factory Fire and instead, I watched a documentary about the Dust Bowl, and guess what...

That documentary gave me a new book idea. So of course, I stopped watching everything about the Dust Bowl and I started watching The Walking Dead, *which gave me a whole new book idea.*

With this new understanding in mind, I've started applying this approach to my own works, including this book. Other than my client's work, every video I am watching right now is a video on writing, editing, or publishing a book. Every article I am reading online right now, as I'm writing this book, is on writing books or designing graphic novels: anything that helps an author share their story with the world.

Am I scared that I might accidentally plagiarize one of them? Nope, not at all. In fact, most of the time I don't even get to *finish* watching that video because I get inspired to get back into this manuscript instead. Surrounding myself virtually with visual reminders of what I'm trying to accomplish here is helping me stay on task and get this done.

And besides, none of them are telling my story. So how could I plagiarize?

In recent years, I have come across hundreds of new authors wondering if they can possibly write a book with ADHD or if they should stick to writing short stories that they can finish before a distraction comes in. That is definitely one avenue you can take. But if you have ADHD and a dream of writing a full-length book, most of the advice out there regarding time management, discipline, focus, and planning are based on neurotypical processes. I encourage you to take some time and reflect on what it is that helps you pull into a hyper-focused mode, what it is that motivates you, and how you can restructure your process to help you harness your ADHD to write the book you want.

Your ADHD is not your weakness. It's your superpower.

Learning to Ignore Your Inner Editor

Most authors I have met fall into one of two camps:

1. Edit as you go. These are the authors who will try to correct as much of their book as they can while they are still writing the rough draft.
2. Right first, edit later. These are the authors who will put off editing, until after they have finished writing.

Just as with nearly every other process out there, neither of these is better than the other. It's not a choice between which one works and which one doesn't; it's a choice of which one works *for you*. And it's probably going to take some trial and error to figure that out.

I'm going to put it to you the same way I put it to all of my clients: if you were to hire me to edit your book, and the very next day I showed up at your house and propped myself up to read over your shoulder to correct you as you wrote, how would you react? If I questioned every single line you wrote, how long before you kicked me out?

"Is that really the word you meant to put there? Is that where that comma goes? Is there a better name for that city? How many times can one character chuckle here?"

Yet we allow our inner editor to do this to us all the time. The only difference is because it's coming from somewhere inside, we don't recognize it as being the abusive troll of having a 5' 3" human being staring over your shoulder and questioning you out loud.

Now, if I showed up at your house and I started questioning every line you wrote as you wrote it, but that made you feel empowered and motivated to continue making better progress, well, you would be the first; but in that case, I would say your inner editor probably is not a big problem at all. Or you have your inner editor in check.

The point here is editing is one *step* in the process, but it does not typically overlap with writing. Editors get the manuscript after the writer is done with it. There are some exceptions to this rule; for example, you can get a chapter review where you send a chapter to an editor for feedback that you could then apply to the rest of your manuscript. But even then, you have to write the chapter before you can send it to the editor for that feedback.

Finally, writing and editing share a similar skill set, but require very different mindsets and very different approaches to your manuscript, which are best left separate.

Writing requires flow, creativity, and unhindered access to your imagination. Editing requires a systematic approach to seek out areas that need improvement to make the story stronger. You can't make a story shine if the story isn't there, and you certainly can't take a systematic approach to a story that isn't there.

Now, I am not saying that you absolutely have to finish your entire book before you can start editing at all. What I am saying is to separate your editing time from your writing time. I mentioned earlier that I do almost all of my writing through writing sprints now and I keep the editing separate. I might do a line edit on a day when I am not doing any writing at all. Or I might take a break after three writing sprints, and then that afternoon sit down to do a copy edit on everything I completed through my sprints.

What I do not do is correct my spelling while I am writing. Even in dictation, if I forget to enunciate the T in writing and end up saying "riding," I'll leave it there until I am done with my sprint. Then, when I have finished my last sprint and I am out of writing mode, I can make the necessary shift into editing mode so I can go back and adjust or correct anything that might have snuck through.

Keeping spell checkers and grammar checkers turned off while I am writing makes a huge difference. All of those red and blue lines showing up just call my attention to the fact that my manuscript might have mistakes in it. Even if it's not a mistake, because sometimes Microsoft Word and Google docs both have issues with certain phrasing, it still pulls my attention away from my writing for at least a few seconds.

Remember what I said about ADHD, those visual reminders are imperative. Follow one red line, and it will lead you to the next red line, and then the next red line. And before you know it, there is a real chance that you have accidentally slipped right out of writing mode, spent all of your time editing, and made no progress with the book itself.

This is also why the chapter on editing is a separate chapter from the chapter on writing.

The Perfect Time to Start Marketing

My heart always sinks a little bit whenever a new author comes up to me beaming with excitement and tells me that they've just published their first book and that now they need to learn how to start marketing so they can start selling copies. If you wait until after your book is already published before you start marketing, you are going to launch your book to crickets and spend the rest of your life trying to catch up.

But if you're new to marketing, it's hard to figure out what to say when you don't even have a book to sell yet (or a release date, for that matter). So how can you start marketing?

It feels like a paradox, right? You have to start marketing before you finish writing the book, but you don't have anything to sell until after you finish writing the book. To solve this paradox, let's take another look at what marketing means.

Whenever I talk to a new author about book marketing, they usually say something along the lines of "I am so bad at marketing, I can't sell anything." This leads me to believe that they don't quite understand the difference between marketing and selling. The truth is, there are three pieces to book sales that a lot of new authors get mixed up: marketing, promoting, and selling.

Let's start with selling, that's the easiest to define. Selling the book, or anything for that matter, involves the actual transaction taking place. The customer sends money to the bookstore, the bookstore gives the reader their book. You could even use the term selling for things like email marketing: a reader gives you their email address, and you send them the free chapter you promised. If it involves the direct exchange of value, that is the transaction which is a *sale*.

Next, promoting. Promoting your book is the process of letting your audience know that you have a book for sale and how they can purchase it. This is the moment you are asking the person to make the purchase and giving them a link to the bookstore or to the website where you have the form that they can sign up for their free chapter. If you do a good job with the *promotion*, then people are already convinced to buy your book before they reach the bookstore, where they can finish the transaction and actually get the sale.

So, where does that leave marketing? Marketing is everything that leads up to the promotion. Marketing is showing up in front of your audience, letting them connect with you, and letting them learn about you as a brand, as an author, and as one of them. *Marketing* is what you do to earn the right to promote your book.

Think about it. When you walk into a party, and someone approaches you and introduces themselves as *Jane Doe, would you like to buy their book*, how eager are you going to be to buy their book? And then, if every time you walked by Jane they were still asking you to buy their book, how long would it take before you stopped making eye contact? Jane Doe isn't interested in connecting with you in a real way. They aren't even interested in whether or not you are their ideal reader, or if you would like their book. They haven't spent any time engaging with you at all: they just want you to purchase their book.

At the same party, imagine if another author, Janet Smith, came up to you and started talking to you about your favorite book, and then started talking to you about their favorite book. And then the conversation moved into what their favorite movie adaptations were. And then, when you ask them what they do for a living, they let you know that they're an author, and their next book is actually coming out pretty soon, and to celebrate they are giving away a free chapter to anyone who's interested. That is much less creepy. Even if you say no, because of money, reasons, or timing, you don't feel like just another number. You feel like there was a connection and had the budget or the timing been just a little better, you might have actually gone ahead and signed up.

That is the power of marketing.

And there are other things to consider as well. Have you ever had someone contact you out of the blue, someone you haven't seen in years, and all they wanted to do was let you know they were selling something and wanting you to buy it?

It's not the request that feels like a letdown; it's the fact that they came out of the blue only to make that request with no lead up. They never really *earned the right to ask you to buy* anything.

If you start marketing while you're still writing, you can connect with your readers and skip all that. But it might be hard to figure out what to say, so I wanted to give you this content bank and tracker, which you can make a copy of by scanning the QR code below:

SCAN ME

As you write your book, you're going to add some amazing quotes, jokes, and life lessons that your audience is going to eat up. These are the types of one-liners that people share across social media because they make them feel clever or motivated. Which means these are the perfect quotes to create graphics out of publish.

Whenever these quotes come up, I like to keep them in a content bank like the one above so I don't lose them while doing any rewrites or edits later. Don't worry, you're not carving them in stone or anything—if you share a quote and then later adjust it a bit, just go ahead and make your change in the tracker. No one will even notice if the quote that you shared was tweaked once the book came out, and sharing the updated quote will help solidify the new quote for you.

You can think of this as sort of putting the pieces of your trailer together. Think of the last time you watched a movie trailer. They show some amazing scenes and quotes in that trailer, but not all of them make it into the final cut. The closer you get to release day, the more accurate the trailers are.

Of course, there is going to be more to building up your audience and marketing your book than sharing quotes from your book. We'll cover several of those strategies later in the book when we talk about marketing. But because marketing is so important and building up your audience while you're still writing your book is so effective, I wanted to make sure to at least pop in here to help you start.

Surviving

The Editing Phase

Surviving the Editing Phase

You did it! You finished your book. At least you finish the first draft, which means you've finished the hardest step of this entire journey.

You already know there's a lot more work to be done. But now you've also proven that you can get it done, you've already done the hardest part. So, congratulations are in order and don't forget to pat yourself on the back.

Now it's time for step two: make it good.

The Editing Mindset

Let's start by talking about what an editor is and what an editor does.

An editor is someone who reviews your manuscript and uses their expertise in storytelling, story structure, market demand, and publishing trends to highlight areas of your book that can be improved. These improvements might include word choice, sentence structure, scene inclusion (or exclusion), pacing, character arcs, overall plot and theme, as well as plot holes and tension.

They are not necessarily there to catch spelling errors or mistakes in punctuation. Don't get me wrong, I have never met an editor who will leave a word misspelled on purpose simply because they weren't there to check for misspellings, but they are there to see whether or not your book delivers the reader experience you are after. And if it does not deliver that experience in the best way possible, they are going to figure out why and they are going to recommend changes to help you fix it.

It's also important to remember that finding an area within your story that could use some improvement is not the same thing as saying that you are a bad writer or that your book is a bad book. I firmly believe that *if you get your story drafted, you are a good writer.* An editor cannot edit anything if there is no story there. Therefore, the fact that you have words on a page, even if it's just a chapter, means you are a good writer.

And besides, no editor wants to receive a manuscript and not be able to do *something*. We want to help you succeed, we want to help your story shine, and we do not want to waste your time or money. And you don't want us to waste your time or money. You don't want to receive your manuscript back from an editor and have to question whether or not we even did anything at all because there were no suggestions or changes at all.

All that said, and the editing process can be an intense one, filled with just as many ups and downs as the writing process. Reading and rereading your story over and over again can start to warp it in your mind. Waiting for that feedback to come back from the editor can make you start to overthink everything.

So let me put your mind at ease: you already did the hard part, right? You already wrote the book. You downloaded your story out of your brain and into a document. Now, you're just going to make it good.

This is where you're going to add in the foreshadowing, the plot twists, and the cliffhangers that your readers love. Where you'll come up with the perfect title and tuck away any loose ends.

Is Your Story Boring?

You probably hear it all the time: you have such a unique story. You're such an inspiration, you should share your story. Your story is so inspiring to others, it could help so many people. This is actually one of the catalysts that spark interest in writing a book for a lot of authors.

Every time you overcame a struggle, every time you spoke to your friend about that one crazy teacher who didn't like you in school or that one friend who almost got you killed, or that one terrifying ex-partner who took off out of your life in the most dramatic way possible. Every major struggle is followed, almost immediately, by a crowd of people who will tell you, "Wow, you should write a book!"

I 100% believe that you should be writing your book and getting it out there. And by the end of this book, if I have done my job, you are going to believe in your story enough to write your book and get it out there.

About a third of my clients have a message they feel compelled to tell—some wisdom they want to impart to their readers. A lot of times this message comes out of their own struggles, a real turn-your-pain-into-your-passion moment. They built something, learned something, or overcame something and they know other people are facing that same obstacle. Their entire goal is to write a book that helps their readers overcome the same struggles.

A few of my clients just have a story in their heads—they just want to see a character or a world come to life. These clients typically didn't get to see themselves represented in the world as they were growing up, and they want to change that for future generations.

But the majority of my clients were told by someone at some point in time that they had an interesting and unique story to share and that they should write a book. And so that's what they set out to do. They set out to write this book because their story is so amazing that someone else told them they should.

You are going to have an impact on so many people because of your book.

And yet, so many authors I have met over the years struggle, either while they are still writing their book, or once they move into the editing phase, because they suddenly feel as though their book—their story—is boring.

Your Story

Is Not Boring,
It Is Inspiring

Why are they struggling so much? And how can their book be boring if they have already been told how powerful their story is?

Once again, it's just their anxiety and their mind lying and playing tricks on them.

Let me tell you something: *your story is not boring*. Your story is not boring or drab or inconsequential. Your story is amazing.

Your story is *inspiring*.

Inspiring enough that someone told you it needed to be a book. Your story is going to help someone heal from something that happened to them years ago or it's going to help someone discover a new strength they didn't know they had or it's going to help them learn something new they didn't think they could do a year ago.

But the problem is that as the author, you're not exactly in the best place to be able to judge how exciting (or how boring) your story is.

Have you ever watched a movie, and it was the most original, exciting movie you had ever seen? It had you sitting on the edge of your seat the entire way through, with just the right number of surprising twists and familiar scenes to keep you interested and engaged.

When you watch the movie again, does it have the same effect?

It might.

In fact, there are plenty of movies I love that I have seen over and over and over again. And I love it every time I see it. The surprise is gone. I no longer jump when the R.O.U.S. (Rodents of Unusual Size) jumps out and attacks Westley in The Princess Bride. I no longer cry when Artax sinks into the Swamp of Sadness in the Neverending Story.

I cry before the horse sinks because I know it's coming, but that's a whole other point to be made.

These iconic plot points are still just as important now as they were the first time I saw them. There's still just as much drama and excitement poured into the scenes as there was the first time I saw them. The scenes have not changed...

I have.

I have become familiar with those scenes and have been able to brace for the attack and mentally prepare myself for the sinking.

Your life story follows the same rules. It doesn't feel as exciting and new to you because it's no longer new. You've lived it. You've learned how to brace for impact with certain things and you've learned how to mentally prepare yourself for other memories. And the same is true when you are writing fiction, presumably a story you haven't fully lived through. You are still obsessing over every scene, every battle, every conversation, and every character introduction throughout your book. You have written, revised, rewritten, read through, and revised again every chapter in your book: of course, it feels overly familiar to you.

It's not that your story is low impact or boring at all, it's just that you've already seen it. Your readers, on the other hand, won't have the same problem. When they read your book for the first time, it will really be for the first time. Most of them won't have any idea what's coming.

And if you're writing nonfiction, the people in your life who were a part of your story and helped to shape your story, will be seeing it now for the first time from your perspective with your insights. So even if they were right there with you, it will be like they are reading it for the very first time.

There's a thing that our brain does which is amazingly helpful (except for when you're trying to write). And that is the fact that it distorts our memories.

Now you may not think of this as being overly helpful but remember: our brain is built to help us survive. And it does that by latching onto and enhancing the memories it thinks are important to our survival, discarding the rest, and filling in the gaps with learned knowledge. Things we might've picked up along the way from our conversations or reading other books or taking in other stories.

But the brain doesn't stop there. I hate to say it, but you are not a good judge as to how exciting your story is. It is just not something you will ever be able to judge fairly because you've lived with it for so long. You've been obsessing over and thinking about every scene and event in your book—fiction or nonfiction—for so long, it's ingrained in your memories to the point where it has been distorted from the exciting reality you've lived through into the boring rerun you've seen a billion times.

So, when I say that your story is amazing and that it needs to be told, I'm not saying that because I want you to like this book or run to leave me a 5-star review. I'm not saying that out of some fake smile or because I want you to turn to the back of the book and find out how you can hire me to be your book coach. I am saying this because I truly believe you need to hear it: your story is *amazing* and it needs to be told.

If your story feels boring to you, then it's only because you've been living with it for your entire life.

Unfortunately, the deeper into the editing process you venture, the more you will probably struggle with this issue. Editing often requires several read-throughs, each of which has the effect of seeing your story *yet again.* This is one of the reasons hiring an editor can help save you so much mental anguish.

Another key point about all of this is subjectivity. What some people think of as boring, others think are exciting or even thrilling. Sometimes this can be altered through our experiences: the person who rode the same roller coaster 7 times in a day might not describe it as exciting as the person who is about to get on for the first time. But anything subjective is hard to evaluate and measure. Which is another reason why it's probably time to bring in another set of eyes.

If you're really struggling with the pacing and excitement of your story, but you're not ready to hire an editor, consider finding some alpha readers to read your story and give you some preliminary feedback. Bringing in a new perspective, a fresh set of eyes, can help you see your story in a different way and find ways to make it work.

There are a lot of resources out there to help you figure out the pacing and excitement of your story. I also have a story self-assessment worksheet that you can work through by scanning the first QR code below. And if you're writing a memoir, I have a self-assessment for your memoir that you can work through by scanning the second QR code on this page:

Your Title Says It All

I am going to preface this by confessing to you that *I suck at titles*.

OMG I am so bad at picking out titles that it is comical.

I spend hours upon hours going back and forth between possibilities, crying and raging over which one is better and why it's not the one I actually like. Of all the skills that go into writing and publishing a book, I have never mastered the art of crafting the perfect book title.

In fact, the folders on my computer and on my backup drive, those 38+ works in progress? The majority of them currently have titles like "*the one with the werewolves,*" "*the one with the vampires,*" "*the one with Jack the Ripper,*" "*the one about the triangle shirtwaist factory,*" "*the one about a time traveling musician,*" and "*the one about the dust bowl…*"

You get where I am going with this: my working titles sound a lot like the titles of an episode of *Friends*.

Luckily, as a ghostwriter, I'm not usually the one who has to come up with titles. Most of my clients come to me with a title already in mind, and because so many of my clients work in business and marketing, their title has already been vetted and researched. Meanwhile, for all the reasons we discussed earlier, most of my books are still sitting at various levels of completion. Even the ones that have titles I like have not gotten to the stage where I have completed any sort of marketing research or keyword research to see how they would perform.

And my first published book, *Everything I Need to Know About Parenting I Learned from Watching Star Trek*, I was stubbornly married to that title. The book sold well, I was very happy with how it did. It sat on an Amazon best sellers list for 3 years in the step-parenting and blended families categories, it was number 1 in parenting, education and number 1 in geek books for a time, and it hit best sellers lists in Japan, Germany, and the UK, making it an international bestseller. So, yeah, even without properly vetting and researching the title, I am very happy with how well it performed.

But I will never know if it might have sold even more copies had I done even the slightest bit of research before settling on that title.

And the real irony is, I would never allow one of my clients to settle on a title without at least researching the possibilities. But you know what they say: doctors make the worst patients.

Yes, your title is as important as you think it is.

First of all, your title is one of the very first pieces of information that a reader is given about your book. They will know the person or website that is recommending the book to them and what that recommendation is based on, such as whether or not they asked for a recommendation, the type of recommendation they asked for, and the keywords that they typed into the search bar online when they started.

Behind that, is the cover.

Well, there's some debate about whether or not a reader will see the cover first and then read the title or read the title first and then see the cover.

That is probably going to depend on the genre of the book, the imagery on the book, the cover, color, scheme, and things of that nature. But at the very least, you can count on the fact that the title is going to be right there in the top three.

That means your title has a very big job to do: it has to convince the reader to click on that thumbnail and read what that book is about. Or to follow that recommendation from their friend and ask for more information. If they are in a bookstore, that cover and title combination must compel the reader to pick the book up and flip it over so they can read the blurb on the back, once again trying to get more information about the book.

Your title is what will ultimately decide whether or not a reader is interested in learning about your book.

You'll also notice that this section on titles is here in the section on editing, rather than in the section about planning or in the section about writing. That's because a lot of times the titles are figured out during the editing phase. Even when you are able to find a title early in the planning phase, like a lot of my clients do, the titles are often changed during the editing process.

Editing is all about finding ways to highlight your story and your voice, to make it more powerful, and more engaging, to adjust the tension, and reflect on the growth that a character goes through during their arc. So, it makes sense that this is the time when you will find that perfect quote, the character's name, the city's name, or the transformation that would make the perfect title for your book.

5 Tips for Choosing the Best Title

1. **Remember the internet is full of contradictory advice.** I'm not kidding; almost every article on choosing a book title will tell you to choose a title that is short and sweet. That makes sense, right? And yet there are books like *A Beautifully Foolish Endeavor* or *Fried Green Tomatoes at the Whistle Stop Cafe* or even *And to My Nephew Albert I Leave the Island What I Won Off Fatty Hagan in a Poker Game* just out there breaking this so-called

"rule" and laughing it up. Accept that there is no one true rule for choosing a book title and be prepared to break a rule if that's what it takes.

2. Check your genre for trending book title formulas or structures. One of the reasons readers rely on titles so much is because the title helps them understand what the book is about. Nonfiction titles like *The Year of Yes* and *Limitless* give their readers an idea of what they are going to learn as they read these books. Meanwhile, titles like *Queen of Coin and Whispers* or *The Ballad of Songbirds and Snakes*, or *Children of Blood and Bone* scream fantasy.

3. Check for other books using the same title. This is one of the biggest sources of frustration, but you can probably understand why you want your title to be as unique as possible. If there is another book using the same title, try to do some research on that book before completely crossing that title off your list: is that book in the same genre? Is it a popular book or has it been recently published? Will the existence of that book cause confusion amongst your readers? There is no rule that says you can't use a title that's already been used, but you want to make sure that using it won't backfire on you.

4. Consider your book cover if you have one. If you already have a vision for what you want your book cover to look like, you might want to take some time and start creating some mockups with your title ideas to see which ones will fit the best. You may notice that the title works best if you separate it into a primary title and a subtitle, or you might find you have a little more room that you were initially estimating. Of course, you also might see that certain words in your title just won't work with a particular font, forcing you to change one or the other.

5. Pull something straight out of your story. Something I really love is when I'm reading a book—any book—and I come across a line that makes me realize why the author chose that title. Sometimes it's a revelation, a character's long-lost birthright, or a quote pulled out of some of the dialogue. You also can't fail with using your character names, unique city names, or a nickname.

Surviving the Editing Phase

Need more help coming up with the perfect title for your book? Scan the QR code on this page to find my Title Brainstorming Worksheets that will help you out even more.

SCAN ME

Before You Start Editing...Take. A. Break.

I cannot emphasize this point enough: after you have finished writing your rough draft, take a break. And not one of those breaks where you are off for a couple of days, but during that entire time you did nothing but obsess over your book, talk about your book, and think about all the things going on in your book. You need a real break; a break that allows you to completely reset your brain from the book.

How long of a break you need is going to be up to you. I usually advise about 2 to 3 days per month that it took you to write your book – so if it took you 10 months to write your book, a break of about 20 to 30 days should be just about right. Of course, you can cut this down or add to it as you see fit. If you have another project that you can completely immerse yourself in and will force you to forget about this book for a bit, you can probably take even more time. If you have a deadline looming, you'll probably need to adjust your break to accommodate.

Most people will tell you that taking this break is important so that you can go back to your book with fresh eyes, and that is one part of it. Taking this break has another benefit as well: it allows your brain time to process the fact that you have *finished writing the book* and you are now preparing to shift into the next phase, which requires an editing mindset.

Print Your Manuscript

My favorite method for editing is, and probably always will be, a paper manuscript with a collection of post-it notes, highlighters, and a couple of good pens. You see, the best way to start with an edit is to do a careful read-through of the manuscript, taking notes along the way. This way, you can read through the entire story and see the big picture to get a sense of which areas need strengthening, which areas need to be revised, where your biggest holes need to get filled, and things like that.

If I try to do this read-through on the computer, inevitably I start editing before I have finished the read-through. I will come across a scene and start adding clarification to it or adding in more details, forgetting that in another couple of chapters, I had already addressed this. This creates double the work because as I work my way through the manuscript, I end up accidentally rendering something in my story redundant or unnecessary, and then I have to go back and change whatever I had just revised, or I have to change even more stuff further down the line.

Of course, if you have written a full-length book, roughly 40,000 words or so, then printing out a manuscript can end up costing you a lot of money to do it at home thanks to how expensive ink and paper are. It can even cost you a lot of money to go to a service like Kinko's and ask them to print it for you. And with either of these options, you are left with a loose pile of papers that, if you've ever had kids playing near your desk who have knocked over a pile of papers, you know, has the potential to be lost and fallen hopelessly out of order.

The most cost-effective method I have found for printing out my manuscript is to actually use a self-publishing platform called Lulu. Lulu has a privacy setting you can select so your book remains private; essentially, Lulu will be your printer only. The purpose of this setting allows you to build a strategy based on in-person orders—you could go to Lulu and order a bundle of books without those books having to be public on the website. But I find this feature invaluable for editing.

So, I log into my Lulu account, I set up a new project with the manuscript, and I throw up a fairly nondescript cover if I don't already have a cover design in mind, select my trim size to be 8 1/2 x 11 inches, be sure to select print only so that an ISBN is not required, and I order myself a paperback proof copy of the book.

And what I receive is a manuscript that *feels* like a book. The pages are bound together behind a cover, but the manuscript is still formatted at 8 1/2 x 11 with double spacing so there is plenty of room for me to make my comments, highlight areas that need revisions, and take notes of any corrections I need to do.

This step of reading through the manuscript before opening it up as a document on the computer has saved me countless hours of editing. Plus, since I have to wait a week or two for the book to print and be sent to me, that helps ensure that I am taking a much-needed break from the manuscript. Altogether, depending on the length of the book, the printing cost is usually somewhere around $4-$5 plus the $4 or $5 to ship the book to me. It's not free, but I have spent a lot more money than that trying to get ink into my printer or heading over to Kinko's and asking them to print me a copy.

Hiring an Editor

You have probably heard more than one horror story about a bad editor out there. In nearly every writing group discussion I have ever been in, there is at least one author with a story about how an editor completely erased their voice from their book, about how an editor took their book and ripped it off, or about an editor who charged thousands of dollars only to disappear without doing any work on the manuscript at all.

Some of these stories I'm sure have happened; others, I think might just be exaggerations. But the truth is, I wasn't there, so I don't know. Every editor I have met, whether new or experienced, has the same goal of helping their author succeed. Acquisitions editors at publishing houses want to see their authors succeed. I have never met an editor who would even think about stealing that "million-dollar book idea" from their client. They would rather be recognized as the editor for that million-dollar book idea.

So, yeah...I think a lot of the stories are false. Most of the time, I hear these claims being repeated by someone who wasn't even involved in the story at all, it was always "a friend told me that she heard about..."

But that doesn't mean that there aren't bad editors out there or that you won't end up with an editor who is a bad match for your book. Differences in perspectives can lead to a conflicted relationship with your editor. So, when it comes to hiring an editor to do a professional review of your manuscript, either to prepare your book for publication or to prepare your book for submission to an agent, here are some of my best tips to help you find the best match.

Start your search at Google or LinkedIn. There are plenty of places where you can find some really great editors. And if you go into a writer's group and ask them about editors, they will start flooding your comments with who they recommend. But if you are going to run a search, search Google for the term "[genre] book editor" and start sifting through the results.

Now, the first page on Google is probably going to be dominated by sites like Fiverr and Upwork. These are not bad sites, but I do not like to start searching there because they do not provide you with the best tools to help you find the best editor for your book. Most of the profiles look exactly the same and give all the same promises, and there are thousands of them. This is fine if you are an experienced author and know what to look for, but if this is your first book and you are about to hire your first editor, trying to sift through pages and pages of profiles to find a good editor will feel overwhelming and pointless.

Instead, skip page 1 and start looking at page 2 of your Google search results. Take notes of some of the editors who have come up. Check out their LinkedIn profiles, look at their website, see if they have a portfolio or a blog online, and start compiling a list of some of the editors you would like to meet and how they can be contacted.

Please note, I am not saying that Fiverr or Upwork are bad sites. And there are a good number of editors who are on LinkedIn and have their own site who work through Fiverr and, upon your consultation, they will send you to their Fiverr profile to hire them through that site. If that happens, that is perfectly fine. I am not against using Fiverr or Upwork to be the communication hub between you and your editor. I am only warning against using those sites as your initial search for an editor when you don't yet know what you're looking for.

Sign up for a free consultation with every editor on your list that you can. Most editors offer a free consultation so it shouldn't be that hard to do. This consultation is usually a video chat that lasts about 15 to 30 minutes where you can talk a bit about your needs and some of the specifics about your book as well as ask them a lot of questions.

Take advantage.

This consultation is for both of you. The editor will use this consultation to get to know more about you and your book and to estimate a time frame in which they can help you. And this consultation gives you the opportunity to learn more about your editor's process and to determine whether or not they are a good fit for your book.

Ask better questions. Most of the authors who sit through a consultation with me end up asking some very basic questions:

- How long does the editing process take?
- How much will this cost?
- What format should I send you the manuscript?

There's nothing wrong with these questions—they're good questions. But they aren't really going to tell you everything you need to know about the editor.

If you really want to know whether or not you're talking to the right editor, get them talking and change your energy a little bit. Ask them things like:

- Why did you get into editing?
- What are some of your favorite genres to edit and why?
- Who are some of your favorite characters and why?

These questions and nothing to do with your book really, and the answers to these questions almost don't even matter. But watch the editor as they answer these questions for you.

Specifically, watch to see if the editor is matching your energy. If the editor can match your energy, they can match your voice and style.

If you have a preferred style guide or notes on voice, send it to your editor. If you are about to drop hundreds or even thousands of dollars on an editor, then they better be the *best* editor for your book, right? You don't want to receive a manuscript back that sounds nothing like the story you are trying to share, that sounds nothing like *you*.

But it can happen. Even with a good editor it can happen.

In 2010, I received a message from an author who was in the same writer's group on Facebook that I was in. I was always such a fan of this author. She already had several books out, most of them self-published, which I had read and loved. She was very active in the group and was always so helpful for everyone in there. And here she was messaging *me*—a virtual nobody at the time. And asking if I was available to edit her book.

And I will never forget her message: "*I understand if you're busy. All the best editors usually are.*"

My heart skipped a beat right then and there. She thought I was a good editor?? Just based on the advice and conversations inside this group on Facebook?

I was so ecstatic over this, I pushed other clients so I could meet with her the next day and I offered her a discount. I wanted to make *sure* I got to edit her book.

There was nothing that I wanted more than to impress her. So I dug into her book with ferocity. Correcting errors, suggesting changes, rearranging entire sections, restructuring chapters…I spent far more energy and time on her manuscript than I normally would have. But it had to be perfect, absolutely perfect.

When I finished, I sent her back her manuscript and I waited. And I waited. And I waited.

Finally, after about two weeks, I wrote her an email checking to make sure she had received her manuscript, and she wrote back and said "*yeah. Thanks.*"

I didn't know what to make of this, but I figured if there was something wrong, she would let me know. She was still posting in the group and commenting on others' posts. I tried to convince myself that I was overthinking, that she was just busy and that's why she seemed as though she'd stopped talking to me.

Finally, she emailed me and asked for another consultation. We hopped onto Skype and she was visibly uncomfortable.

That's when she told me that she was upset with me and the way I had edited her manuscript. She was so upset that she had actually tried to hire another editor. But this second editor advised her to come back and talk to me before they would take on this manuscript.

You see, in my zeal to catch *everything* and make this manuscript *perfect*, I had completely removed her voice. Instead of sounding like a Black Woman from Louisiana wrote the book, it sounded like a White Lady from Connecticut wrote the book.

I felt awful. To this day I still get embarrassed whenever I think about it. It's every editor's nightmare to be told that they erased someone's voice out of a manuscript. And thank goodness we were able to work together, get it fixed, and produce a book she was proud of that *sounded like her*.

My point is, things like this can happen. We were able to fix it because she talked to me about what elements were her voice. And now, I make it a part of my process to ask about these things during the consultation. But not every editor is going to think to ask about things like this. They are going to edit your book in accordance to the style guides they know best (usually *Chicago Manual of Style*). You can save yourself a lot of headaches by talking to them about these style guides and ensuring they understand how to keep your voice in there.

Self-Editors, Listen Up!

There is a lot of debate out there about whether or not authors should edit their own work in lieu of hiring an editor. There are people who believe authors cannot possibly do as good a job editing their own work as a professional editor would be able to do. Some say the author is too close to their story while others say the author doesn't know how to edit.

I believe any author *could* self-edit their books, but they have to understand that self-editing is not the same thing as writing, and self-editing is very different from hiring an editor. That might sound like a given, but it's a little more complex than it sounds.

When you self-edit your book, you are losing a couple of distinct advantages that hiring an editor would be able to provide you, and you have to acknowledge those differences so that you can make up for them in a different way.

First, for those who say that an author is generally too close to their story to be able to self-edit, this is not that far off from the truth. This is one of the reasons why I recommend taking a break. It's also one of the reasons why I recommend not pushing to publish your book too quickly after you have finished writing it. Hiring an editor can take anywhere from 30 to 90 days to get your manuscript back, depending on the length of your book, and then you would still be looking at 3 to 6 months of back-and-forth revisions before the book is ready to be published.

This means if you finish writing your book in January, you are doing yourself and your book a serious disservice by trying to self-edit that book and get it pushed out by February. In fact, I would not even choose a publication date at all until the self-editing step is complete, just to ensure that you are giving yourself enough time to learn and implement everything you need to know to edit your story and make it shine.

Proper self-editing is always slower than hiring an editor. If it takes a professional editor 2 months to edit your book, you can probably expect to spend 3-4 months editing your book. Part of this is simply a difference in professions—the more often you edit, the faster you get at editing. But part of this is the fact that you have to take breaks in order to create distance between yourself and your story.

Your editor gets to review your story with a fresh perspective outside of your own. And while they will do their best to match your voice and your vision for your story, they are also able to bring their own expertise and perspective in to help determine whether or not certain parts of the book work for your vision. This is where an author's proximity to their story can hinder them.

If you are too attached to the words on the page, you struggle to replace them with better words.

Second, editors bring that all-important feedback. The feedback might be based on industry knowledge, market research, their own years of expertise in the genre as well as current trends. Editors know how books sell and they know which books are being picked up by publishing houses. When you are self-editing, you are cutting out a vital source of feedback that could help you improve your manuscript.

Once you understand these two elements that you would be cutting out of the editing process, now you can put together a self-editing plan to help you work on these two aspects and improve your editing.

I've put together a self-editing checklist to help you get through the process smoothly. You can grab it by scanning the QR code below:

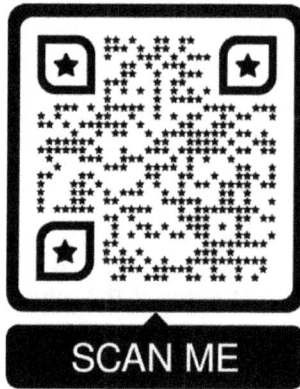

SCAN ME

Step-by-Step Editing Process

During the initial read-through of your manuscript, start by looking for the obvious issues:

- Problems with the story flow.
- Inconsistent character presence.
- Plot holes or major inconsistencies within the plot theme
- Obvious loose ends.

What you're doing here is making sure the story stands on its own, that the foundation you laid out is solid enough that you can build on top of it and not have everything fall apart.

Next, it's time for your first round of feedback. To do this, look for Alpha Readers. These are readers who are going to understand that your book is still in the pre-publication phase and needs extensive polishing. You can find alpha readers in many writers' groups, which is a great source because you know they have experience with storytelling. You will want writers or editors to have experience with your genre.

Your alpha readers are going to look for all the same things you just went through to find: plot holes, problems in the theme, troublesome scenes that don't seem to fit, as well as areas in the book where the story seemed to lag or seemed hard to follow.

While your alpha readers are going through your manuscript and sending you that much-needed feedback, you should be taking another break to help reassert any distance that was lost during your round of editing.

Once you have the feedback from the alpha readers in your hands, it's time to take their feedback, read through it and make any adjustments to your manuscript that you see fit.

Congratulations, you've just completed the Developmental Edit. The structure of your story is done.

It's important to note here, whether you are receiving feedback from editors or feedback from alpha readers, feedback is made up of suggestions only. At no time should you take the feedback to mean anything absolute. If you don't agree with it because you feel it will damage your story rather than enhance it, then you can absolutely choose to ignore any of it.

Next, if you have the need for sensitivity readers, now is the time to start gathering them. Sensitivity Readers help provide feedback based on character development and respectful representation, especially if your book contains characters or events that you do not have an intimate knowledge of. For example, if you have a character dealing with a traumatic experience that you have never experienced, it would be helpful to get a sensitivity reader to read through your manuscript and give you feedback on your handling and representation of that traumatic event. The same for bringing in characters of other ethnicities, other genders, and abilities.

I like to have the feedback from the sensitivity readers come in after those major rounds of developmental editing so they can see the full foundation of the story. If the Developmental Edit is *what* the story says, then the sensitivity readers are the ones helping you with the tone of *how* you said it.

The feedback from your sensitivity readers will go directly to your next round of edits, which is the Line Edit. As I just said, sensitivity readers help you with the tone of your story, and that is what the Line Edit is all about: tone.

- Overall emotional reaction to the story.
- Each character has a unique presence.
- Each character uses a consistent voice and tone throughout.
- Overall mood and tension of the plot builds and seeds appropriately.
- Use micro cliffhangers at the end of chapters to compel the reader to keep reading.
- Add in or adjust scenes, transitions, chapter hooks, and time lapses throughout the book.

The Line Edit ensures that the story invokes the emotional experience you're after with the book. That the tear-jerking scene jerks those tears, that your jokes are funny, and that the couple you want your reader to route for is worth rooting for.

After the Line Edit, we come to the third round of editing, which is the Copy Edit. The Copy Edit is probably the type of editing you had in your mind, as it is the most common form of editing. The Copy Edit goes into sentence structure and word choice.

Remember back when you were writing your book and you were worried that you just couldn't seem to do your story justice? That you couldn't find a way to describe pancakes without saying the word pancakes?

This is what the Copy Edit was made for. Your Developmental Edit strengthens the foundation of your story, your Line Edit highlights and strengthens the tone of your story, now the Copy Edit makes sure you are choosing the right words to do your story justice.

- Use an active voice whenever possible.
- Remove filler words like that, just, very, and really.
- Remove adverbs or replace them with the more appropriate verb.
- Double-check for commonly mixed-up words like affect and effect.
- Consistent spelling and capitalization of proper nouns.

- Variable sentence lengths that create a pleasant reading experience and facilitate the tension and emotion you are after.

Now, you might be wondering why you can't just go through your manuscript and check for all of these things all at once. Why not check for adverbs at the same time that you're checking for plot holes and why not fix a character arc at the same time that you are checking for filler words? Once again, this comes down to trying to remove the need for extra work.

It's a lot harder to edit for tone and emotional response if the structure isn't solid. It's like trying to hang pictures on a wall before the house has been built. Sure, you can probably do it, but you will find that the photo is probably going to fall and you are probably going to have to move it several times before you can finally hang it where it belongs.

Applying the Feedback After Hiring an Editor

This is it! This is the moment you've been waiting for. Your dreams, all your hard work, and all those hours spent writing and revising your book have culminated at this moment: the moment you receive that all-important feedback from the editor you hired to review your book.

You open up that email and download that document, eager to read all the positive comments, the oohs and aahs, and just how much the editor loved your story.

And then your heart sinks.

Instead of oohs and aahs, your manuscript is filled with comments, red marks, green text, insertions, entire scenes marked as "unnecessary", and several paragraphs of analysis you don't know how to interpret.

Let me start by telling you this: I warn every single one of my clients that the more commentary they see from me throughout their manuscript, the better. It means that I am drawn into their story, it means that I am invested and making their story the best that it can be, and it means that they have succeeded in pulling me into their world. Yes, believe it or not, all those red marks are *good*. I don't know when or why the myth started that editing is only for bad writers, but I want to put an end to it right now.

Of course, being taken aback and surprised by the amount of feedback on a manuscript makes complete sense. First of all, this is your book, it's your baby, it's your legacy. You wrote this book with all the passion you could muster. Your entire being is in this book—and for some authors, their entire identity is wrapped up in that book. Second, you've spent weeks or even months writing this book. Putting in countless hours of research, writing, rewriting, and editing all before sending it over. You probably expected it to be perfect, or at least as perfect as you could get it.

So, who the hell am I, a ghostwriter and editor who was not around as you were pouring your soul into your manuscript, to tell you that your story wasn't as good as you thought it was?

Despite my upfront warnings to be prepared to see feedback, most of my clients are still surprised by the amount. Some have confessed that they believed their book would be the first to cross my desk and need very few revisions, being that they spent so much time self-editing the book. Others thought I was exaggerating the editing process. Others expected me to correct the occasional typo, or throw in a comma where they happened to miss one and were thrown off when I questioned the presence of a character within a scene.

And then there's the actual feedback itself. Most editors will provide a write-up of several paragraphs or even pages where they explain to you their analysis of your manuscript. And the analysis is great, it is very informative, and if you want to know what went into each of their recommendations, as well as how you can make your writing stronger and cleaner in the future, that analysis is golden.

It's just not always very tactical. And because this analysis usually appears at the end of the document, it can be hard to line up certain pieces with the changes that have been tracked within the document itself. Fortunately, most editors will also include a summary of action tasks you can take to apply their feedback. Other editors, myself included, will send you a second document file in which they've already accepted their recommended changes to give you a chance to see a cleaner version of your manuscript along with their commentary.

Just as I did when you started your round of self-editing, I recommend that you read through your editor's feedback before touching anything.

Start with their analysis and then read back through every comment they left that explains why they are suggesting certain changes. Have a notebook and pen at the ready as you read through this feedback to take notes about what they have said. And don't forget to note down any feedback you deeply disagree with as well as the feedback you plan on following.

What I like to do next is review my notes on the editor's feedback and reflect a bit on my thoughts regarding everything.

- What kind of impact would this change mean on the manuscript?
- How would this change affect my readers' experience?
- Does this change bring the book into alignment with my goals?

I think a lot of times authors pour so much of themselves into their book that they are afraid taking on too much of the editor's feedback will erase their voice rather than enhance it. And there are some instances in which that will happen. Aiming to be 100%, grammatically, correct, for example, is a surefire way to remove your unique voice from the manuscript.

Trust me on that.

By reading through the feedback, first while taking notes and then reading through your notes, you have a chance to create a bit of distance between you, your story, and the feedback. This gives you a chance to really take a look at what each change is going to mean for your book and for your readers. Then make a decision regarding how you want to address each of the suggested changes.

Ultimately, I hope you chose your editor because you trust their judgment; but even then, that doesn't mean you're going to agree with everything they said. You may choose to follow the editor's recommendation, you may agree with the editor's thought process but disagree with their recommended solution (thereby coming up with a different solution to fix the issue), or you may choose to reject the recommendation altogether. As you make each decision, keep the reader's experience in mind.

I have not met an author yet who, even while disagreeing with my feedback and choosing to go their own way, broke their book irreparably and ruined their reader's experience. As long as you keep the reader's experience in mind, I believe *you* will make the best decisions for your book. And in the end, that's what we all want: we all want our readers to get that positive impact from your story.

Proofread, Proofread, Proofread!

You might think that, after all of these rounds of edits, your manuscript would be perfect by the end of it, right? Certainly, after all the feedback from alpha readers, sensitivity readers, and editors, after being reviewed by other writers in the field, by being read, over and over and over again by yourself, applying all this feedback and improving your manuscript that you would catch every single rogue comma and misspelled word in there.

Allow me to be the bearer of bad news: there is a reason proofreading is a completely separate step from editing.

Through each of these rounds of edits, you have turned your story into a page-turning book. Now it's time to go through with a fine-toothed comb and make it error-free. If you like, you can use an AI editor, such as ProWriting Aid or AutoCrit, to help you spot a lot of these errors.

I know there is a lot of debate about whether or not an AI editor can do the same job that a human editor can do, and I don't think they can—but I don't think they're meant to. The proofreading step is where AI editors are really going to shine. They are going to help you pick out the tiniest of errors, misused words, and misplaced commas. Run-on sentences, and all those other little mistakes that were persistent enough to slip through each of your other rounds of edits.

And if this step feels like it goes on forever, that's because it does. Take this book—so far I've edited, I've hired an editor, I've edited again, I've hired a proofreader…and I'm *still* finding mistakes to fix! I almost feel like it could be a game at this point: how many typos can you find?

Anyway, congratulations! After countless hours of staring at your manuscript, and right when you think you can't read it one more time, you are finally ready to move on to the publishing stage.

Traditional Publishing and Editing

If you have chosen to get your book traditionally published, your editing process is going to look somewhat different. This is because once a publishing house picks up your book, they will be overseeing the rest of the publishing process instead of you: editing, formatting, proofreading, cover design…all of it.

I still recommend doing at least that first round of self-editing. Check for those plot holes, check that the character arcs are complete, and look over the structure of your story. However, this process is less about getting your book ready to publish and more about getting your novel ready for an agent or an acquisitions editor to review. There is no requirement for you to go through rounds and rounds of revisions, nor is there a requirement for you to hire an editor before approaching agents about your book.

The one thing I will say is that it is always best to put your best book forward. If you send a manuscript out to an agent, and that manuscript has never been reviewed or edited (by you or anyone else), you are significantly increasing the chances of rejection.

I have heard from a couple of authors who told me their agents prefer to receive unedited manuscripts so that they can see the raw talent available in a pre-polished manuscript, but I *haven't ever heard an agent corroborate* that. In twenty years of working as a ghostwriter and editor, every agent I have ever had the pleasure of talking to has recommended doing at least one round of edits yourself if not two or three. And the reason for this recommendation is so that they can see the story the way you see it. The writing phase was all about downloading the book out of your head and onto paper. Using the words you had. Agents and acquisitions editors need to be able to review your manuscript quickly to determine how well they are going to be able to sell it. The more plot holes, the more inconsistencies in themes or character arcs, the more filler words bloating the word count and the harder it looks to sell. At that point, it looks like it's going to take a lot of work to sell even if the story is amazing.

And if it's going to take a lot of work before they can make it sellable, that's a lot of money they have to sink into trying to fix it up.

So, if you want to give your book its best chance at finding an agent and being picked up by a traditional publisher, I recommend taking the same break as you would if you were self-publishing, then perform at least one round of developmental edits on the manuscript itself. Clean it up, fill those plot holes, make sure every scene is compelling, and that the characters are each pulling their weight, and then you're ready to start querying.

Dare

To Be Published

Dare to be Published

Publishing comes with its own sources of fear and excitement. Now it's becoming even more, real—the book is done, it's been edited so much that you're tired of reading it, you've applied every ounce of feedback you've received so far, and it's time to finally get ready to share it with the world.

This is it...this is the dream, right?

And now you're just thinking, "*who the heck was going to tell me that getting my dream was going to feel like a brick hitting my stomach?*"

If you haven't already made up your mind between self-publishing and traditional publishing, this will be the time to start really going over the advantages of both and what they can offer your book.

Self-publishing offers speed and full control over the entire process. Instead of being the author, you become the publisher. On the other hand, traditional publishing offers the backing of a credible company and someone else to take the reins over the publishing process so you can concentrate on marketing your book.

Of course, there are other advantages to each publishing path. And there are a myriad of considerations to go through when it comes to making your choice.

I've put together a worksheet to help you choose between self-publishing and traditional publishing, which you can grab by scanning the QR code below:

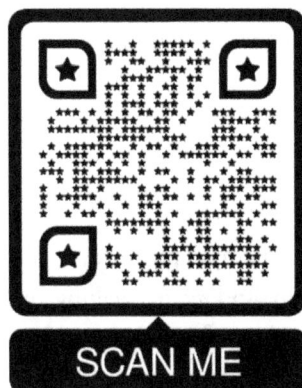

SCAN ME

I want to make something else really clear as you go through the worksheet and consider your options. A lot of new authors seem to be under the impression that if they go with traditional publishing, that the publisher will handle all or most of their marketing for them. But this isn't necessarily the case. Your publisher may be able to help you with some of the marketing or they may be able to point you to a few different resources, but regardless of the path you take, you are going to be shouldering the majority of your marketing through your launch and beyond.

How Do You Know Your Book is Finished?

One question I hear all the time from new authors, and especially from Pantsers, is, "*how do you know when that book is finished?*" How do you know that it's time to stop writing, stop editing, and start querying agents or formatting to get the book published? It's a great question, and the good news is that it's not as difficult as you think.

If you are writing fiction, you want to start by examining the opening of your story. What situation was your protagonist in? What was your protagonist's personal motivation and goal? And what was the state of the world in your story? The end of your story should look like the mirror image of that beginning image: the protagonist should be outside of the situation they started in, looking at it from the new perspectives gained throughout the story. The protagonist's personal motivations and goals should have been fulfilled as applicable; and the state of the world should have been addressed to reflect the protagonist's changed visions.

For non-fiction authors, you can go back to your original purpose for the book. Did you answer all the questions you set out to answer? Does your book deliver on each of the promises you are making to your readers?

Once your book is done and polished, if all you're doing is reading through it again, and again, and *again*, making tiny changes each time that is more about a personal preference or seeking perfection instead of strengthening the story or fulfilling a goal, then it's time to move on. The good news is, if you are going for traditional publishing, then you know that your book is going to cross paths with at least one or two more editors down the road, so there's no reason to be pulling out your hair right now. And if you are self-publishing, then you have the advantage of being able to fix anything after the fact.

I am not saying that you should get sloppy or purposely put out a bad book just because you can fix it later. But it is a pretty cool safety net to know that if you do happen to find one more of those extremely sticky typos, you can easily update your manuscript and swap it out in your book in less than 24 hours, allowing you to fix it and virtually no one needs to know.

On the other hand, if you are writing a non-fiction book and a couple of weeks after your book comes out, you discover some new information that you wish you had put into your book, or you got a new case study that would have been perfect for this book, or anything along those lines at all, you can always write it into your manuscript, and release it as a second edition.

In other words, while you are working to put your best book forward, there is no reason for you to be driving your mental health into the ground striving for perfection.

The Two Biggest Fears in Writing a Book

I've heard just about every reason and fear that anyone has ever given about writing a book, but there are two that always seem to be right at the top of the list:

1. What if no one reads my book? Is it worth it to put in this much effort for no one to bother reading it?
2. What if everyone reads my book and it's *bad*? Can I bear the embarrassment of having to face someone I know who doesn't like my book?

What if no one reads your book

In the summer of 2019, I was facing a little bit of a conundrum. Video marketing was on the rise, and I hated it because the video was always so hard for me to do. I have a very small space to work with, a lot of clutter in my house, kids, and animals to work around, and it was always loud. I had to set up lighting, put on makeup, declutter the area behind my cameras, test out different angles, and I never was really all that confident about showing my face on camera anyway.

There's a reason why my first brand was *The Invisible Author*.

Then I was scrolling Facebook one day when I happened to see a live video with an amazing person, Molly Mahoney, and I paused to see what she was doing.

She was *showing up*.

I think for that particular Livestream, the most viewers I remember seeing at one time was five. And at one point, she looked at the camera, she said, "*I have two people here right now who need me right now. Business is about showing up for your audience on their time, and you can't control when your audience needs you. The only thing you can do is to show up for them anyway. And when they need you, they will come to you.*"

When I tell you that this one piece of advice absolutely changed my life…

This advice has been etched into my soul. In fact, I sent her a friend request soon after watching that live show because it has made such a huge impact on me—the idea that when you are showing up for business you are showing up for people who are going to show up on their own timeline.

And her energy never faltered. It made no difference to her whether she was talking to two people or two hundred people, she was there for *them*. It doesn't matter how many people watch your live presentation, what matters is that the presentation is out there for anyone who needs it when they need it.

On that same token, it doesn't matter if your book sells hundreds of copies on the first day, what matters is that the book is there when people *need* it to be there. You have a message to share with the world, and the world will show up to read it once the world is ready.

But until then, *you have to show up*. You have to plan, write, edit, and get that story out there.

If you are worried that you are about to publish a book no one wants to read, welcome to the club. This is probably one of the most common fears that I hear from authors and clients.

And let me ask you something else… What *if* no one reads your book? So what? Would that really be so bad?

Would that prove that your book was bad?

So many authors have this expectation built up that if no one reads their book, then it must be bad. But here's the thing: if no one reads your book then that is only a sign that *no one is reading your book*. It has absolutely no bearing on how good the book is.

Now, you could make an argument that if no one reads your book, your marketing strategy was bad. But there are plenty of bad books out there that are hugely popular and continue to get new readers every single day. There are plenty of bad books out there that have movie deals because they are still so popular.

Even years after they came out and changed the ratings.

Popularity has absolutely nothing to do with quality.

Write your book because it needs to be on the bookshelf and ready for when someone needs it down the road.

What if everyone reads your book?

Back in 2015, I was getting ready to walk the stage at my graduation ceremony with my Master of Arts degree in psychotherapy, and the first draft of my parenting book, *Everything I Need To Know About Parenting I Learned From Watching Star Trek,* was sitting at home waiting for me to design a cover and upload to Amazon.

By this time, I had already been ghostwriting for 13 years, and I had helped 3 of my professors write and publish their books that year. So, I was confident in my knowledge of the system.

What scared me was how many of those same professors were going to see my book and read it, knowing that they had been in discussions with me about parenting—some of them had taught me about parenting. And I had family members who were asking me about my book and when it would come out because they wanted to read it.

I hadn't even let my own husband read the draft yet.

It seemed like I couldn't go anywhere without someone asking me when this book was going to come out. And I hadn't even done any marketing. In fact, I didn't even realize that so many people in my life even knew the book was coming out, that's how little I felt like I talked about it.

And every time I went to hit publish, I got scared: what if they all get disappointed in this book? What if every person I know and love reads this book and they hate it? How would they tell me? Would they tell me?

How would I face them?

How could I go back to ghostwriting for clients?

Or go back to parenting my daughter?

Eventually, I hit publish. And, just as I had feared, the book started selling.

And I avoided everyone.

I stayed off-line and pretty much just holed myself up in the kitchen baking crème brûlée's and merengues all day. After all, they can't tell me they hate it if they can't find me in the first place. My messages on Facebook were being flooded, my email was being flooded, and my text messages were flying through. And yet I ignored them all because I knew I wouldn't be able to handle it if they didn't like the book.

Well, they did like the book. After about six hours, it was number 1 in kindle books on parenting and number one on step-parenting and blended families. In fact, it stayed in the top five on Amazon for step-parenting and blended families for three years.

Of course, if I were anyone else, I would've been telling myself to grow a thick skin. That not everyone has to like your book, and even mild discussion, even criticism, is good and healthy. I've had that discussion with so many of my clients over the years, it's practically second nature for me. And in the back of my mind, I knew that.

Yet I still wasn't ready to hear what people thought of my book.

There was just something different about feeling like everyone in the world was about to read your book and form opinions on it. It's one thing to publish a book and understand that it means it will be going to market and that means people will be reading it, but it's completely different when you *know* that this is going to happen because people were already asking you about the book.

If the thought of running across someone who has read your book gives you anxiety, welcome to the club. You are in good company.

Authors pour a lot of their hearts and souls into their books. There is a huge level of reflection and insight that ends up inside every book they write. So, it makes sense that when an author comes across someone who has read their book, they are not always going to be ready to hear that person offer up their own interpretation and thoughts about their very soul.

It's just not something many people are ready to do.

Ultimately, this anxiety comes out of a fear of embarrassment and judgment. For many authors, writing no book at all is better than writing a *bad* book.

In fact, this fear can sometimes be so bad that it will stop people in their tracks.

Back in 2016, I had a client who paid thousands of dollars to have me help them develop and write their book. They went on to pay another editor thousands of dollars to edit that book. Then, somewhere amid the marketing research for a book cover, they ran out of confidence in their idea and completely gave up.

I still think about that book sometimes, wondering if the author will ever recover their confidence to put it out there. But I digress.

Fear

Can Help You Make
Sure Your Book
Delivers On Its
Promise

If you follow me anywhere on social media, then you know that I am a big fan of Doctor Who—have been since I was a child and Tom Baker was offering up jelly babies. And one of the things I learned from watching Doctor Who was that fear was sort of like a superpower: *"Fear can make you faster and cleverer and stronger...But that's okay because if you're very wise and very strong, fear doesn't have to make you cruel or cowardly. Fear can make you kind."*

As it turns out, there's something else fear can help you do: Fear can help you make sure your book delivers on its promise.

Go back to your goals that we drew up at the beginning of this book:

- The goal you wanted to achieve.
- The reader experience you wanted to provide.
- The promised skill or impact you wanted to include.
- The premise you designed.
- The genre you chose.

If you hold true to each of those things, you have nothing to be afraid of. If you find that some of these things are missing, use the time you have before you publish the book to go back and put them in. No one will ever be the wiser.

You Can't Please Everybody, Can You?

I don't know if you've noticed this before or not, but readers are people. And people have feelings, emotions, political beliefs, religious beliefs, prejudices, biases, gender identification, and a whole lot of baggage. And every time we sit down to write a book, one or more of these things come into play.

It's like I said earlier, we pour a lot of our heart and soul into every single thing that we write. This includes all of this baggage, it can all come out in a variety of ways. But when that baggage happens to land on one side of a controversial topic, that's when things can get a little bit rough. That's usually when authors tend to get scared of their book idea.

So, how can you write a book, especially a book that touches on difficult subjects, and not offend anyone?

The quick answer is that you can't.

Someone is going to get offended, that's just the way of the world right now. We all have such ingrained beliefs—they make up who we are. And when those beliefs are challenged, we get defensive. It's almost as if our very identity has been challenged. So the chance that your book is going to offend someone is not a possibility, it's a given.

But that's not the question you should be asking. The question you should be asking is *who*? *Who* is your book going to offend?

Two topics in particular I am asked about all the time when it comes to controversial topics is racism and having an LGBTQ-plus character. Every time, the person asking me the question is a relatively new author with no name to back them up, and no huge author platform to carry. They don't have a lot of the fame and fortune that helps back up big-name authors. If these people find themselves on the wrong end of a scandal, it will ruin them.

I feel bad that so many authors have to worry about things like this—why can't we just share our stories with the world and the people who relate to the stories read them and those who don't can just keep scrolling?

But we all know they won't keep scrolling, so here is the advice I tell everyone: do you really care if *those* people are offended? The people who were never going to like your book anyway? The people who refuse to keep scrolling because they just have to stop to say something mean when *they're* offended?

Go back to your ideal reader and consider whether or not *they* would be offended by your book: as long as that answer is *no*, you're good! Publish your book.

You aren't setting out to please everybody, you're setting out to please the *right* people. Sometimes this might mean curbing your language a bit, or it might mean leaving certain things out, but other times it means screaming your truth loud and clear for all to hear.

And have you noticed, sometimes a little controversy actually ends up bringing more attention to your book—your ideal readers will start defending you (and your book) against the people who were never going to read it anyway but who just hate the topics, and that brings up more attention.

How Long Does the Publishing Process Take?

As I mentioned before, if you choose to go with an agent and traditional publishing, the publishing house will be in control of the schedule of release. But you can probably estimate about a 2-year timeframe between the moment you get signed and the moment your book hits the shelves. Of course, there are always exceptions to the rule. I've seen books hit the shelves in just a few months. In fact, when Rachel Pedersen wrote her book, *Unfiltered,* she finished the draft in April, and the book was released by Hay House in September of that same year.

If you are self-publishing, you get to control the release date, which means you can wait as little or as long as you like to hit the button and publish your book.

I recommend giving yourself a runway of about 3 to 6 months after your book is done editing. This way, if you haven't been able to concentrate on building your author platform or marketing your book just yet, you have a chance to do so before your book is actually out. This also helps relieve some of the pressure so that you can get through those last few steps for formatting your book, check with your beta readers, finding reviewers to check out your book, getting the cover design, not to mention actually getting your book up onto the platform.

Preparing Your Book for an Agent

The other day, I was sitting on TikTok doing my weekly chat on writing and publishing a book and someone asked me a question, *"statistically speaking what were her chances of finding an agent and getting published?"* And I said 100%.

100%.

I said what I said.

Right now, you're probably yelling at me. You're probably ready to throw this book and start quoting all those statistics you've seen about how hard it is to find an agent and how so many authors have their manuscripts get rejected and never get published. I've even seen people quoting that the acceptance rate of agents is close to like 2%.

How can your chances of being traditionally published be 100% if the acceptance rate is barely 2%?? That doesn't even make sense, right?

It doesn't help that there are still writing coaches out there saying things like *"if you can't find an agent then you can always fall back onto self-publishing"* as if self-publishing was a consolation prize for the unpublishable.

Here's the truth: if you have a book and you want to go find an agent and get it published through a traditional publishing process, there is a *100% chance* that you will live out that dream. **But only if you *do* it.**

I have never met an author who has tried everything within their power to get traditionally published and was *not* able to land that deal.

Don't get me wrong, having a 100% chance does not mean that it's going to be easy or that you won't have to live through any rejections. I have met plenty of authors who went out and tried to get traditionally published and were unable to land that deal. But the one thing that they all had in common was that after so many rejections, they gave up. They did not take the feedback and apply it to their query letter, their book proposal, or their manuscript to try to improve anything. And most of the time, they were sending so many query letters out at the same time, they were receiving dozens of rejection letters all at once.

So they gave up. They *decided* that their dream of traditional publishing was out of reach. They *decided* that they weren't good enough.

You are not going to make that same mistake because you are going to go through these tips to build a strategy for querying agents rather than just sending your manuscript out to anyone and everyone.

Make sure you polish your manuscript. I touched on this a little bit in the section on editing, but let's go a little deeper this time. You are not aiming for perfection. At this point, you do not need to be stressing out about hidden plot holes or missing major structural pieces. If you find them, definitely fix them; but there is no need to drive yourself up the wall and or pull your hair out hunting for these things. If you give yourself a good enough break and do a solid read-through and the first round of self-editing, you will find any egregious errors that you need to address.

There are a couple of little tricks you can do to help make sure you catch most of those annoying little typos. First, change the font size and type of your manuscript. So, if you wrote the manuscript using Times New Roman size 12 font, switch it up to Arial size 10 or something. Then start reading through everything. The new font size and type force your eyes to process everything as fresh data, which helps you catch things you might otherwise miss. It's kind of like how you will send an email or publish a post on social media only to find a typo right after; the font used on the published post is always different from the font used inside the edit screen while you are writing the post.

You see, as you are writing, your eyes and your brain both become very familiar with your work, and with that familiarity comes the risk of glazing over your words rather than reading them and spotting the errors. We tend to edit what we *think* we wrote rather than the actual letters on the page.

Another little trick you can do is to read your manuscript out loud. This trick will actually help you catch more than just typos, you will also catch repetitions, areas that are difficult to read, and sentences that just don't make sense. Once again, by changing up the way you are inputting the data of your manuscript, you are forcing yourself to have to process everything as new, which increases your ability to capture things you might otherwise miss due to familiarity.

And make sure no part of your manuscript could qualify as a "rough draft". I see this happen with authors all the time, and I myself am guilty of this mistake quite often. What happens is as we are going through the manuscript and making our changes, we don't go back and reread the section that received those changes. In its basic definition, that section is now a rough draft—meaning that it has not been reviewed or even proofread.

And wouldn't you know, but most of my mistakes and typos happen in those areas: the areas I rewrote and added in *while* editing but failed to go back and reread after.

So, if there is any part of your manuscript that you did a significant rewrite in, or if there are any paragraphs or sections that you have added to your manuscript through the editing process, make sure you go back and spend some extra time rereading those areas.

Next, you are going to want to gather the names and contact information of several agents. I did say that your chance of being traditionally published was 100%, but that percentage is dependent on a number of things, and it does not mean that the very first agent you submit to is going to accept your manuscript. So, head over to manuscriptwishlist.com or agentquery.com and start putting together a list of agents who work with your genre as well as their agency and their contact information.

Once you have a list of 20 to 30 agents, start visiting their websites and taking notes of how they want to be contacted and what they want included in your submission. Agents are very particular about their submission process for a reason, and you want to make sure you are paying attention and following their instructions. Most agents will list the format of your manuscript and your letter, acceptable delivery methods such as email attachment or file type, and they will even give you their average turnaround for responses.

This is where I like to create a calendar with my clients and put together a schedule, starting with their dream agents and working our way down, to decide when to reach out to which agent. For our first round of submissions, we usually send to no more than two agents– one if their dream agent wants an exclusive submission. Then we wait an appropriate amount of time to hear back from the agent.

Once we have an answer from that first round of submissions, we revisit the query letter and the manuscript, and we submit to the next two to three agents and we wait. Yes, querying to agents can be a long and arduous process, but doing it this way helps ensure that your best query letter is always the one being sent out and that you're not receiving a whole bunch of rejections all at the same time, which can be devastating to your mindset.

What Goes into a Query Letter or Book Proposal?

Depending on the agent and genre, you may be asked for a query letter, which acts as a sort of cover letter to your sample chapters, or you may be asked for a full book proposal. Either way, these submissions need to answer a few questions:

1. **What is your book's meta-data?** Meta-data is all that information such as title, genre (i.e.., Fantasy or Romance) and population (i.e.., LGBTQIA+), age group (i.e.., Young Adult or New Adult), and word count that will help your agent classify your book. If your book is following several points of view from different characters, you'll also want to clarify that it is either multi-POV or dual-POV.

2. **What is your book about?** Be sure to cover your character, their primary conflict (both on a personal level and within the story arc), and what's at stake. This is the time to be hooking the agent and making them excited for this book, so don't hold back anything here thinking that they can discover more later.

3. **What marketing research have you already done on this book?** This is where you would list any of your comp titles as well as describe what your book brings to the market.

4. **Who are you?** Be sure to answer the question *"why are you the one to write this book?"* You can also add why you want to work with this particular agent as well as information about your author platform such as

how many followers you have on which channels and what your current rate of growth is.

The more clearly and concisely, you can answer each of these questions, the better. This can seem a little tricky, trying to cram all this information into an email of about three-four paragraphs. Remember that agents are human beings with hundreds of submissions to review coming into them every day. They don't want to read your life story, but they do want to know if your book is a good fit for them.

I also want to take minute and point out that a book proposal might serve the same function as a query letter, but they are not the same thing. Book proposals contain more in-depth information about you, your book, and your market as well as sample chapters. Additionally, most book proposals are written and sent out before the actual book has been written.

Query letters are more concise and may or may not include sample chapters depending on the agent you're sending it to.

If you are writing a nonfiction book and are wanting to be traditionally published, then I recommend learning how to write a solid book proposal to help you land that agent before you get too far into your book. Typically, once you have about 50 – 60 pages of your book written, you have enough to start putting together your book proposal.

Applying Feedback from Agents

If you hear back from an agent that they are rejecting your manuscript, congratulations! I know that sounds sarcastic, but a lot of authors sometimes go without ever hearing any feedback about their manuscript and are forced to move on without actually even being told yes or no by agents. So, receiving a rejection still allows you to move in a direction. It's even better when that rejection includes specific feedback about your manuscript, but that can't always happen so we take what we can get.

Once you get over the initial feeling of hurt about being rejected, read over the feedback, and try to put together a picture of how you can apply it to your manuscript. Sometimes, that feedback might not feel readily applicable or tactical. For example, I had a client once who was writing a historical novel based on events in South Africa, and she wanted to remain true to the people in that area at the time, so she used a lot of those surnames. When she received her first rejection from an agent, the feedback praised her for her writing and for the story, apologized that they weren't quite the right fit, and then informed her that the character names were not meaningful to modern-day readers.

It's sort of vague and confusing at first, right? How can names based on historical events be meaningless to modern-day readers? Why does it matter?

This is when she came to me because she wasn't sure how to use that feedback to improve her manuscript. The truth is, when readers today are reading a book based in 1912 and they keep seeing names like Smith or Miller, it's not overly meaningful even though those names are popular and were popular back in 1912. This is the same thing, substituting common South African surnames in place of Miller and Smith. When we went through the manuscript and replaced those names with other authentic South African surnames that had meaning, it gave a whole new level of depth to those characters and to the plot as a whole.

This does not mean that feedback from an agent should be taken as gospel; just as when you receive feedback from your alpha readers or from your editor, these are suggestions only based on their years of experience and expertise. So, I would not recommend dismissing the feedback without thought, but you definitely do not need to pull your hair out if you don't agree with the feedback.

What if the Agent Does Not Send You Feedback or Does Not Respond to You at all?

If the agent does not send you specific feedback about your sample chapters or your manuscript, this is a sign that your query letter or book proposal was weak. This is when you will want to revisit your query letter and edit it to make sure it is compelling, to the point, and clearly answers the questions above.

If an agent cannot understand what your book is about, why you think they are a good fit, or what potential this book has out on the market, they're probably not going to read much further into your proposal. You also want to make sure you take the time before your next round of submissions to ensure that you are following the agent's submission guidelines, using (and spelling) their name correctly, and that you are sending your query within their open window.

Why do Agents Care about Your Author Platform?

Agents consider a lot of factors as they review a manuscript. Most of these factors help them predict the overall sales success of the book. If everything adds up to a predicted success, they'll sign on. On the other hand, if all these factors don't add up to success, they will pass until the time comes when that mass is different.

It goes without saying that the most important factor in a book's overall success is the strength of the story. Not even the writing, because the writing can be fixed and edited later, but the overall plot and development of the story. The character growth, the themes, the perceived impact, and value inside that manuscript: if you have that, you already have a good shot at success.

The next biggest factor in a book's success is the author platform you have built up before querying. Your author platform is the proverbial stage from which you tell the public your book is available. This is where people will meet you for the first time and hear about your book, and where many of them will decide whether or not they want to buy your book.

If you are self-publishing, your author platform will be your most important tool for the success of your books, but you can choose to publish before the platform is built up if you like. Because agents and editors will want to review your author platform, you'll need to start building it up before you start querying. In fact, as I mentioned earlier, you'll need to start building it before your book is even written. But if that gets to be too hard to balance out, then focus on writing the book first and start building your author platform up while you're getting ready to query (just push back querying a bit as you do this).

As far as how large your author platform should be, that's all up for debate as well. I have heard other book coaches say that the agents they know prefer to see authors with 100,000+ followers online, which seems to be backed up by some of the articles out there. However, most of the agents I have met over the last few years have all agreed that they would rather see an author with 5,000-20,000 followers who are highly engaged than a large, bloated following.

And yes, 5,000 followers might still seem like a lot, but believe me, it's easier to reach than you might think as long as you are focused on your readers' experience and tapped into what they want to see online.

All that said, the size of the following isn't the most important factor of your author platform—the connection is. If you have a following of any size and it looks like they connect and engage with you and will likely buy your book if you tell them about it, then you have what it takes to impress many agents out there.

Adding the Final Touches

You are so close to being finished with your book now, I bet you can taste it. All that's left to do is to finish polishing everything up, grab some final bit of feedback, and you are ready to roll.

Formatting

If you're traditional publishing, you're going to want to check your agent's submission guidelines to find out how they want your manuscript formatted. If by some chance they do not have formatting specifics, then you can play it safe with standard formatting:

- Times New Roman Font.
- Size 12.

- Double spaced (please use the spacing settings to set this; do not use your Return or Enter keys to add in these extra spaces)
- 1-inch margins all around.
- Page breaks before each Chapter with the Chapter Heading sitting about ⅓ down the page (do not use the Return or Enter keys to add move your Chapter Headings to a new page, instead insert the Page Break, then move the Chapter Heading down the page to give room for commentary).

If you're self-publishing a book, then you're doing more than just preparing your book for an agent to read and comment on: you're getting ready to present it to the world! It's important to properly format your text to ensure that it looks professional and is easy to read. Here are some general guidelines to follow:

1. Use a clear and easy-to-read font, such as Times New Roman (for print) or Arial (for eBook), in a size between 10 and 12 points.
2. Set your page margins to at least .87 inch on all sides (this might vary depending on the size of your print book). This will give your reader some white space to rest their eyes and make the text more comfortable to read.
3. Use a consistent and easy-to-follow layout for your chapters and sections. This could mean using a standard font and size for chapter titles or using headings and subheadings to organize your content.
4. One space after punctuation marks; the exception to this is at the end of the paragraph where you will have no space after that final punctuation mark. Yes, the whole two-space thing was drilled into my head, too; and yes, it really will make a big difference in how your book looks and reads. One space.
5. Use justified text alignment, which means the text will be aligned along both the left and right margins. This creates a clean, professional look and makes it easier for the reader to follow the flow of the text.
6. For print books, include page numbers in a consistent location on each page, such as in the header or footer. This will make it easier

for the reader to find their place if they need to refer back to a previous page.

7. Use proper paragraph formatting, including indenting the first line of each paragraph. (Use the formatting tools to do this rather than using the space bar to manually push the line in). This will make your text easier to read and more organized.

8. In nonfiction books, you'll want to add extra space between some of your paragraphs to help your readers absorb all your great information.

9. Of course, make sure to proofread your text carefully to catch any last-minute, stubborn typos or errors. Yes, they are probably still hanging out because those buggers have more staying power than my favorite lipstick.

Beta Readers

I am going to start off the section by letting you know that the term *beta readers* means different things to different people.

Some authors and coaches use the term *beta readers* to refer to what I called *alpha readers* earlier: those initial readers who will provide feedback on plot structure, character development, and the overall quality of the book so you can consider their feedback and apply it as you move through the editing phase.

Other authors and coaches, myself included, use the term *beta readers* to refer to a similar group of readers with a very different purpose. Like alpha readers, beta readers are usually volunteers who will accept your manuscript to read and provide feedback. The difference is in the type of feedback the beta reader will provide.

Unlike alpha readers, who provide developmental aid to your story, beta readers are providing *your first glimpse into market reaction.* They are the ones who will tell you whether or not your story met their expectations, whether or not it worked for them, and, overall, how much they loved it.

Now, I am about to say something, highly controversial: *your beta readers should love your book.*

Gasp.

The typical advice is that not everyone is going to love your book, beta readers included. And that you should be happy to receive negative feedback about your book at the beta reading stage. I disagree.

First of all, if there is going to be any negative feedback regarding the development of your manuscript, you should have received that already from the alpha readers, the sensitivity readers, and any other editors or proofreaders you have consulted about your manuscript. The time for negative feedback is over.

Beta readers are for *market* feedback, which means you should be targeting readers who match your ideal reader.

If you invite people to beta read your manuscript for you, and they don't like your book, then either you have missed some important feedback earlier in the process or you have asked the wrong person to read your book. If it's the first one, then you will need to go back to the drawing board, revisit the feedback you received from earlier readers and editors, and revisit the application of that feedback to improve your story more. If it's the second one, you will need to revisit your book's North Star and positioning, genre, and who your ideal reader is.

More than anything else, I view the beta reading stage as a real test of your ability to see who your ideal reader is. And it's okay if you are struggling with that, a lot of authors struggle with being able to spot their ideal reader. But, as you can imagine, once you are able to narrow down your ideal reader, your marketing will become infinitely easier. Instead of talking to everyone about your book and wondering whether or not anyone cares, you will get better and better at attracting the people who already want to read your book.

Think of it this way, would you rather go into a large room of book lovers and start talking about your fantasy romance novel and find that about a third of those people are even interested, if they were able to hear you at all over the rest of the noise in the room; or would you rather go into a smaller room filled with people who all love fantasy romance novels, and talk to them about your book, away from the noise? I know which one is easier.

Cover Design

There are a few things to consider when choosing a book cover design for self-publishing.

First, the cover should be eye-catching and visually appealing. This will help to grab the attention of potential readers and make them want to pick up the book. Make sure you are choosing a design that looks good at full size but also looks good when shrunk down into a thumbnail, since most people are going to see the smallest size first while they are scrolling through online bookstores, websites, and social media posts.

Next, the cover should accurately represent the content of the book. For example, if the book is a thriller, the cover should convey a sense of suspense or mystery. If the book is a romance novel, the cover should be romantic and whimsical. I love using a site like Amazon to scroll through books in different categories to start gathering ideas. Besides being an online bookstore, Amazon is basically a huge search engine. You can scroll through all the best-selling books to see what their covers look like, the overall aesthetic each cover conveys, and what they all have in common. Then strategize ways to make your book stand out and look a little different without looking like it belongs on a different bookshelf.

Finally, the cover should be easy to read with clear, legible text. The title and your name (or your pen name if you're using one) should be prominent and easy to find. Along with your title, your book cover is going to be one of the first things they see—it needs to tell them at a glance that this is the right book for them and compel them to click through the page or pick it up from the bookshelf to read the back and learn more.

Scream it

From The Rooftops

Time to Scream it from the Rooftops

This is it! The moment you've been working so hard to get to (I seem to say that a lot, don't I?)!

Your book is finished.

And whether you're headed down the road to start submitting to agents and publishers or getting ready to self-publish, it's time to start spreading the word. But how do you do that?

This is where your author platform is going to come into play. Hopefully, you took my advice earlier and started at least talking about your book a bit while you were still writing it; but if you didn't, that's okay. You can still start building up your audience.

If you are aiming for traditional publishing and are submitting your manuscript to agents, be sure to start building your author platform as you go and update your query letters with your new counts along the way. This way, your query letter will always reflect your latest numbers and you'll be able to see just how much you really are growing.

This also gives you the added benefit of being able to talk about that growth in your latest query letters via a sentence like "*I am currently sitting at about 3,000 followers and am growing at a rate of about 5% per month; I expect to be at 5,000 followers within the next 6 months.*" This type of calculation lets your prospective agent know that you are paying attention to those numbers and that you are on a positive trajectory: two things agents love to hear!

If you're self-publishing and you haven't really started building up an audience yet, I recommend you put on the brakes before you publish your book. I know you're excited to be done with everything and want to see it out at bookstores, even if they are online bookstores. But there's no need to rush the publishing process at this point. The book is done, so you have plenty of time to work on building up your audience before you pull that trigger.

If you really *really* just can't wait to get that book up online, then set it up for a pre-order, but give yourself plenty of time. Both Amazon KDP and IngramSpark allow you to set up pre-orders for up to 12 months. This might actually be the best of both worlds since it will mean you can hit that publish button and still give yourself plenty of time to build up a platform for yourself and drum up some interest.

What Goes into an Author Platform?

A lot of new authors equate their author platforms with social media, but the truth is that social media is just one tool that you can use to build your author platform. If your author platform is the stage that you are standing on, then social media is but one plank holding up the stage. And you can build that stage out of as many planks as you like. There are no rules about which tools you need to have.

Just as with the planning process, the writing process, the editing process, and even the publishing path, building your author platform and your marketing strategy is a personal journey that often differs from one author to the next.

The key to a healthy author platform, whether you are self-publishing or traditional publishing, is to remember *quality over quantity*. You do not need to have a million followers to sell your books. You do need to have followers who are engaging with your content. The old rule of thumb was that you needed 100,000 followers before an agent would consider your manuscript. This number is big and scary and no longer accurate.

As I said earlier, every agent I have spoken to in the past few years has told me that they look at engagement over the number of followers all the time. In other words, it's better to have 3,000 followers with a really high engagement rate that shows your followers want to buy your book than it is to have 100,000 followers built on nothing. So, as you are building out your author platform and choosing your channels, remember that you are building a strategy for connecting and engaging with your readers, not just trying to grow your following. The following will come later.

Layers of Your Solid Marketing Platform

I break down the author platform into three primary categories or layers: your marketing core, your expansion layer, and your local layer.

Your Marketing Core

Your marketing core will serve as the foundation for everything else you do online, so it is essential to have this core set up first. I often refer to the elements of your marketing core as the "*marketing trifecta*" because even if you never expand into any of the other layers of marketing, as long as you have these 3 elements set up and working together, your marketing will be solid. And, once you have these 3 elements set up and running smoothly, expanding into other channels becomes much easier.

1. **Your website.** It does not have to be a huge and complicated website, but it does need to be yours. You need an *About Me* page that introduces readers to you, you need a *Contact* page that helps readers, book clubs, events and librarians get a hold of you, information about your book(s), as well as a form where people can sign up for your email newsletter.

2. **An email newsletter.** Every time I bring up email marketing, someone groans at me because they hate email, yet email is still one of the top online activities people perform every single day. An email has the highest reach out of any channel out there, and this is where people are actively signing up to hear about the updates for your book because they want to know when it's coming out. Authors who use email marketing sell 42% more books than authors who don't.

3. Your favorite social media channel. That's right, one channel, your *favorite*. I know there are a lot of articles out there talking about which channel is the best for which demographic, or which genre—none of that matters. No one is on just one social platform anymore; everyone is on at least 2 if not 3.

That means you are not going to miss your ideal reader because you are on Instagram instead of TikTok. So, choose your favorite, and start there.

With your trifecta in place, now your marketing can be simplified, starting with your favorite social media channel.

Back in the planning stages of your book, one of the things you put together was a picture of who your ideal reader is. Pull them back up and start thinking about them. What do they do when they are on that social media channel? What kind of content are they engaging with? What other authors do they follow? You can even do a little bit of spying and check out other authors who are similar to you—what kind of content are they putting out? Of all their posts, which ones are getting the most likes or the most comments? And how can you re-create the same type of posts but related to you?

Don't worry, I am not telling you to copy anyone. Copying someone's post or stealing their content wouldn't work for you anyway since it would be about them. But look at the type of content that is working for them, and then plan out how you can create the same type of content for your readers.

Next, as you are posting content onto your favorite social channel, your goal is going to be getting your readers over to your website. This means most of your posts on social media are going to end with a call to action to your website.

A call to action is a simple request that lets your visitors know what to do next. For example, if you used any of my content ideas to start posting on your favorite social media channel, and your book is not done yet, you might use "go to mysite.com to sign up for updates about this book."

And, of course, as you are sending readers to your website, they are finding your form right there where they can sign up to be on your email newsletter, which is where you will be sending these updates.

And don't feel restricted to "updates." You can get creative with your call to action:

- Go to mywebsite.com and sign up to receive the first chapter for free.
- Go to mywebsite.com and sign up to get a free book.
- Go to mywebsite.com and sign up for free weekly tips on this subject.

As you grow and build, your calls to action will become more diverse and stronger, but these will at least get you started.

As your email list starts to grow, send out tips, free stories, free chapters, and updates about your book. You can also use your email list to look for alpha readers, sensitivity, readers, beta readers, and even arc reviewers. What better place to look for reader reviews than in your own community of fans?

Your Expansion Layer

After this Marketing Core is built and running smoothly, that's when you can add on the next layer, your Expansion Layer. This is the layer in which you might add another social platform, a podcast, book, influencers with popular blogs, interviews with various authors, magazines, publications, and things along those lines. And again, as you build this layer out, your call to action remains the same: go to my website.com to sign up for this really cool thing I want to send you.

This is what makes having the trifecta set up first so powerful; you can start expanding and your core is already in place to leverage your new audiences. And you don't have to struggle or scramble to try to figure out what to do if someone heard a podcast and suddenly emails you out of the blue. They won't email you out of the blue because you told them to go to your website.

Finally, your Marketing Core is running strong and supporting your Expansion Layer, now you can start venturing into your Local Layer. Your Local Layer includes things like events at related organizations, book signings, appearances at libraries or vendor events, local radio stations, local television news stations, and anywhere in your area where they might interview you and introduce you (and your book) to their audience. With a growing author platform online, you can help spread the word about any appearance in your local area, which makes you a valuable partner.

Obviously, this is a very simplified marketing strategy. There is a lot more to marketing that I couldn't possibly fit into this book because it would double the length. So, I do recommend that you start building out your trifecta now but understand that there is still a lot more to learn about out there.

Building a Launch Team

As you're getting ready to wrap up production on your book, you may want to start putting together a Launch Team. A Launch Team, also called a Street Team, is kind of what it sounds like: a group of people who come together to help you launch your book.

But that makes it sound too easy, right? Just start asking your friends and family and they'll help you!

Well, slow down just a minute.

Yes, your friends and family would love to help you launch your book, but they want to help you launch your book because they love *you*. The best people to recruit to your Launch Team will be people who love you *and love your book*. There might be some overlap, particularly if you have friends or family members who also happen to match your ideal reader, but at this phase it's much more important that you invite people who will want to read *and love* your book.

Once they join your team, people will start trying to spread the word about your book both before the actual launch and for a week or so after the launch. Some things you can ask your launch team to do include:

- Read a copy of your book and leave an honest review at sites like Amazon and GoodReads (make sure you and your Launch Team are following all the reviews best practices and guidelines!)
- Call their local bookstores and ask them to stock physical copies of your book on their shelves.
- Interview you for their own blog, YouTube channel, or social media channel.
- Email their following to let them know about your book.
- Work with you to host giveaways for their audience.
- Take photos of your book (in any format) and post about it.
- Recommend your book to their local libraries.
- Include your book as part of their book club.
- Promote your giveaways.
- Show up at your book signing events (or promote them if they can't show up).

As you can see, there are all sorts of activities your Launch Team can do, and they don't all require a large following to get them done! But they do require a pretty big commitment, so don't skimp out on your Launch Team. Make sure you are taking care of them, providing them with a free digital copy of your book and other goodies or prizes as you come up with them.

You'll also notice that not everyone can (or should) do everything on this list. For example, not every member of your Launch Team will have an email list (although other authors who write in the same genre as you do might). Not everyone runs a blog or a YouTube channel. But any of these activities can have a huge impact on your book's success and overall reception, so make sure you are recognizing everyone on your team equally.

I also recommend you open up a Facebook group to serve as your Launch Team's headquarters. This will make it easier for you to keep communicating with your launch team, send them information and updates, and keep them hyped up and excited about your book.

Make sure you give your Launch Team enough time to read your book if you want them to be able to promote it effectively. Usually, starting your active launch activities about two weeks before your book releases is enough time for them to really hype you up; so, you'll want to send them a copy of your book about two weeks before that (about a month before your book's release date) so they have enough time to get everything ready.

Toast to Your Success

If you've gotten this far, then *congratulations*. You have just accomplished something not very many people accomplish.

Did you know that only 1% of the people who set out to write a book ever actually get one published? And yet, here you are…

Doing the thing.

I don't know if your launch went exactly as you had hoped or if your journey through this process was everything you dreamed it would be. I don't know if you're going to jump into writing another book or if you're still obsessing over making this one perfect. I don't know if you're selling as many copies as you hoped or if you're struggling to get the word out…

No matter what, though, I hope you're as proud of yourself right now as I am of you.

Always remember one thing: as long as you don't give up on your book and as long as you keep your readers' experience in mind, you can never break your book.

Someday, you're going to be someone's favorite author, and I am just so proud that I could be a part of your journey there.

Someday,
You're Going To Be Someone's Favorite Author

Thank You for Writing Out Loud!

I want to thank you, from the bottom of my heart, for buying this book and especially for reading all the way through to the end.

If you have any feedback for me, I would love to hear what you have to say! Your comments will shape any future editions of this book.

Please take just two minutes to leave me a review at your favorite online bookstore, or if you prefer to send me your feedback privately, you can email me at naomi@helpmenaomi.com.

SCAN ME TO REVIEW

www.ingramcontent.com/pod-product-compliance
Lightning Source LLC
Chambersburg PA
CBHW070438100426
42812CB00031B/3329/J